Real Life
to the
Extreme

Real Life to the Extreme

Finding God's Will for Your Life

Bruce & Stan

VINE
BOOKS

SERVANT PUBLICATIONS
ANN ARBOR, MICHIGAN

Vine Books is an imprint of Servant Publications especially designed to serve evangelical
Christians.

Scripture quotations are taken from the *Holy Bible,* New Living Translation, © 1996. Used
by permission of Tyndale House Publishers, Inc., Wheaton, Ill. 60189. All rights reserved.

Published by Servant Publications
P.O. Box 8617
Ann Arbor, Michigan 48107

Cover design: Left Coast Design, Inc., Portland, Oregon

02 03 04 10 9 8 7 6 5 4 3 2

Printed in the United States of America
ISBN 1-56955-200-2

Library of Congress Cataloging-in-Publication Data

Bickel, Bruce, 1952–
    Real life to the extreme : finding God's will for your life / Bruce Bickel and Stan Jantz.
        p. cm.
    ISBN 1-56955-200-2 (alk. paper)
    1. Teenagers--Religious life.   2. Teenagers--Conduct of life.   I. Jantz, Stan, 1952–
II. Title.

    BV4531.2 .B538 2001
    248.8'3—dc21

                                                                            2001003127

CONTENTS

Introduction

The word *extreme* is very trendy. If you want to be cool, you have to be extreme. It doesn't matter what you're doing—doing laundry, taking a nap, or buying milk at the Circle K—you're cool as long as you are *extreme*.

Of course, if you are doing something that has the potential to inflict great bodily harm, then you really are extreme, because by its definition *extreme* means "intense," "severe," "not reasonable," and "sensation seeking." Extreme sports—such as snowboarding, sky surfing, motorcycle jumping, and backyard WWF-style wrestling—fall into this category, and they have become quite popular in our culture. (We wonder why NASCAR, which is also very popular, has not been designated as an extreme sport, since it meets the definition in all respects. We can only guess that it has something to do with the clothing associated with the sport. Whereas most genuine extreme athletes wear loose-fitting clothing that looks secondhand but is in fact very expensive, NASCAR drivers wear tight-fitting jumpsuits with "Mr. Goodwrench" and "Sees Candy" logos emblazoned on them, and that just isn't very cool or extreme.)

The companies that sell you products have been quick to pick up on the *extreme* concept. Take the lowly taco, an ordinary food that's been around for a long time. Eating a taco can be very enjoyable but is not very exciting, unless it's *extreme*. Now, you would think that an extreme taco would be one soaked in sauce so hot that it blisters your lips the moment you taste it. But that's not at all what the taco sellers mean. If the advertisements are any indication, an extreme taco is a taco eaten by extreme people, and extreme people are people who live on the edge or at least *look as if* they live on the edge. In other words, if you are an extreme person—or you look like an extreme person because you have tattoos, body piercings, and a very intense look about you—then just about everything you do is extreme, including eating tacos.

7

What Does It Mean to Live Real Life to the Extreme?

Right here in the beginning of this book, you might be wondering what we mean by *Real Life to the Extreme*. Are we talking about *being an extreme person*, or are we talking about *doing extreme things*?

Actually, this book is about both, because we're going to talk about you and the things you do. You can't have one without the other. You can't separate the person you are from the things you do.

Chapters 1-6: Being an Extreme Person

In the first six chapters we're going to focus on you and the most extreme part of you—God. We're making a pretty big assumption right off the bat, and that's the assumption that you have a relationship with God. Maybe you have decided to make God a part of your life by special invitation, or maybe you aren't quite ready for something so personal, so you are more of a God-seeker. You are spiritually sensitive, but you aren't quite ready to make a commitment.

Wherever you are in your spiritual journey, you have decided to give God some consideration. Good move. Bringing God into the scope of your personal experience is an *extreme* thing to do. You see, without God, you are a mere mortal, an ordinary Joe (or an ordinary Jill), a part of the mundane world. But with God, you enter the world of the supernatural, you are an extraordinary person, you are part of an extreme world. You are an extreme person not because of you or your coolness quotient but because of God.

In Chapter 1 we're going to look at what it means to have God fully open up your life. While everyone else is merely making a living, God wants you to have a phenomenal life. He wants you to be an extreme person.

In Chapter 2 we'll explore the person of God, the most extreme Being in the universe. God isn't Santa Claus or the Tooth Fairy or your Great Heavenly Grandpa. God is the awesome Creator and Master of the Universe who knew about you before the foundations of the earth were laid. As huge as God is, he knows all about you—including the strengths you brag about and the weaknesses you'd rather hide—and he has some extreme things he wants you to do.

Chapter 3 attempts to give you some insights into the age-old question,

"How can I be free to make choices, if God already knows what I'm going to do anyway?" We won't be able to completely explain it, but that's OK. We'll give you enough to expand your mind and open your heart to these wonderful mysteries of God.

Have you ever wondered how to find God's will for your life? That's what Chapter 4 is all about. Some people have the misconception that once you get into a personal relationship with God, he completely takes over your life and your will and pretty much takes the fun out of your life. Not true. God may be the King of Kings, but he's not a dictator. He is your guide. God is extremely interested in who you are and what you do, but he's not going to run your life for you. He simply wants you to follow him.

In Chapter 5 we explore some specific things God wants you to do. It's not enough to *know* God's will. *Doing* God's will is just as important (maybe more so). We give you seven practical principles you can use to evaluate opportunities and solve problems. Remember, God is your guide. He will show you the way, but you've got to make choices every day to follow God's will.

Chapter 6 addresses how to handle the other people in your life who expect to have a say in what you do. As much as you'd like to think that your life is between you and God alone, there are other people out there who have some definite ideas about what you should be doing. All around you there are people with expectations about you—your parents, your friends, your teachers, your spiritual leaders, your business partner, and on occasion the person who cuts your hair. In this chapter we'll show you how to please God without displeasing the people who care about you.

Chapters 7-12: Doing Extreme Things

The next six chapters focus on the extreme things God wants you to do. We're not talking about life-threatening, move-to-Bosnia kinds of things. These are life-changing, I'll-serve-God-wherever, I'm-a-child-of-the-King kinds of things. A lot of people wave their hands at God and say, "Look what I'm doing." We want you to look at God and ask, "What are you doing?" Now, that's an extreme way to live!

Chapter 7 deals with choosing your life's work. How specific is his call on your life when it comes to your vocation? What is the call of God anyway, and how does it impact your career? Are the two mutually exclusive, or can they work in harmony?

When you live life to the extreme, you will inevitably face extreme setbacks. That's not being fatalistic, just realistic. Chapter 8 will talk about setbacks and suffering and what to do when bad things happen.

Choices are a part of the game of life, but some choices are a whole lot bigger than others. Chapter 9 is all about priorities, because extreme living isn't necessarily about living your life to the extreme 100 percent of the time. Remember, life is a marathon, not a sprint.

The last three chapters are where the book gets really good, and we're not just saying that because we wrote them. Chapter 10 is all about the power God wants to unleash in your life—if you will only let him. Prayer plays a major role in this process, which is a little unsettling, because most of us don't pray with purpose, passion, and power.

Chapter 11 is about the "Hall of Fame" believers found in Hebrews 11. Who were these people, and what did they know about extreme living? Check out their stories and find out!

Chapter 12 concludes with twelve principles for finding Real Life to the Extreme. If you keep doing these twelve things, your life will become even more exciting and fulfilling than you ever imagined possible.

What Kind of Book Is This, Anyway?

Our prayer for you is that you would find this book very helpful as you make the choices that matter in your life. We have written *Real Life to the Extreme* so you can learn more about yourself as you learn more about God.

- **This Is a Book About You.**
  We hope this book helps you get to know yourself better as a person uniquely created by God to do some extreme things.

- **This Is a Book About God.**
  We hope this book helps you get to know God better, because the more you know about God, the more you will live your life to the extreme.

- **This Is an Interactive Book.**
  We're not experts, by any stretch of the imagination. We're just two ordinary guys who are a little farther along life's extreme highway than you are. We've done our best to give you practical information and inspiring wisdom to guide you, but we don't expect you to agree with everything we've said. Whether you agree or disagree, we'd love to hear from you, and we promise to respond to you personally. There are several ways to get in touch with us:

  E-mail: guide@bruceandstan.com
  Web site: www.bruceandstan.com
  Snailmail: Bruce & Stan
  P.O. Box 25565
  Fresno, CA 93729

Are You Ready to Live Your Life to the Extreme?

It's time we stopped telling you what we're going to say and start saying it. If you're ready to find out what a *Real Life to the Extreme* is all about, then we suggest you turn the page and start reading. Don't worry, we'll be with you every step of the way.

CHAPTER 1

A Living or a Life:
The Choice Is Up to You

The trouble with the rat race is that
even if you win, you're still a rat.

—Lily Tomlin

You want an extreme life. Don't be afraid to admit it; we know you do. Maybe not extreme in the sense of snowboarding down the slopes of Mt. Kilimanjaro, or jet-skiing the crest of a tsunami tidal wave. But extreme in the sense of living with excitement and escaping the mundane routine of day-to-day existence. We don't blame you. Nobody wants a life that is mediocre, boring, and bland. We all want a life that is exhilarating.

Not too long ago, we traveled across the country and interviewed people about the meaning of life. While we were in Washington, D.C., we spoke with the Chief Operational Officer of a global think tank who told us what she wanted as her epitaph. Don't get the idea that her tombstone was already ordered and that she was on life support. She was in her early thirties and there were no oxygen tubes emanating from her nostrils. This woman was full of life, and that's how she wanted to be remembered—with the following inscription on her gravestone:

This woman did not exist. She lived!

Does that epitaph describe you? Maybe not, but we suspect that you would like it to characterize your life. Unfortunately, however, most of us are more deserving of an epitaph that reads something like this:

He was born. He died. Not much happened in between.

Let's face it. A few people have found the secret to living an extreme life. The others just have an existence that is extremely uneventful and uninspiring. If you are in the latter category and want to break free from a mediocre existence into a life of extreme excitement, then we know Someone you need to go to.

God's Extreme Guarantee

We know that the mention of God may not bring extreme and exciting images to your mind. (We are assuming that stained glass windows, choir robes, and lengthy sermons don't get your adrenaline pumping.) But don't confuse *religion* with *God*. Where faith in God is concerned, some people can get pretty caught up in nonessentials; we suspect that God himself finds some of it boring.

On the other hand, God is the most extreme being you will ever encounter. We'll talk about his amazing character traits more in Chapter 2, but right now let's focus on one very interesting statement made by Jesus Christ:

My purpose is to give life in all its fullness.

JOHN 10:10

To help you grasp the full meaning of that verse, let's look at how it reads in a few other versions:

- *I came so they can have real and eternal life, more and better life than they ever dreamed of.*

  Contemporary English Paraphrase

- *I am come that they might have life, and that they might have it more abundantly.*

  King James Version

- *I came that they may have and enjoy life, and have it in abundance—to the full, till it overflows.*

  The Amplified Version

Does it surprise you that God intends you to have an extreme life? It shouldn't. God is full of intense passion, emotion, and excitement. As Tony Campolo points out in *Carpe Diem—Seize the Day*, the Old Testament Jews knew God as someone who experiences intense emotions:

- He can be angry (see Deuteronomy 6:15).
- He is merciful and compassionate (see Exodus 34:6).
- He jealously protects the worship that belongs to him alone (see Deuteronomy 4:24).
- He can change his mind when moved by love and pity (see Exodus 32:11-14).
- He rejoices in his creation (see Psalm 104:31).

Although Campolo doesn't use the word *extreme* to describe God, we think he would concur with that adjective. Campolo reminds us that God was pleased with David's spontaneous act of worship as he wildly danced before the Lord (see 2 Samuel 6:14). Campolo also points to the Song of Solomon as an example of the passion of God: the writer of this book uses graphic expressions of love that blur the line between communion with God and sexual ecstasy. Come to think of it, God was the designer of marriage and invented sex for pleasurable intimacy between a husband and wife. How extreme is that?

There are many dimensions to this "life with all its fullness" that Jesus promised. Of course, it includes eternal life (see Romans 6:23), but it also means being relieved of the burdens and cares that weigh us down and sap all of the enjoyment out of life:

> *Then Jesus said, "Come to me, all of you who are weary and carry heavy burdens, and I will give you rest."*
>
> MATTHEW 11:28

And it means that God wants to give us direction and purpose in our life so we aren't wandering through life dazed or in a fog:

> *Jesus told him, "I am the way, the truth, and the life."*
>
> JOHN 14:6

God's grand design for your life includes the promise and potential for an extreme life.

So Why Are We Stuck With a Mediocre Existence?

There seems to be a common malady that afflicts much of the human race: mediocrity. It is as if some virus infected our systems and rendered us incapable of excitement and enthusiasm. We live our lives as if we have been quarantined in the hospital's isolation ward. We have been promised a vital and vibrant life but have confined ourselves to a drab existence of bedpans and Jell-O.

Henry David Thoreau recognized this malady (although he missed the clever hospital analogy) when he said:

Most men lead lives of quiet desperation.

For the Christian, this is a depressing state indeed. Christ promised us "life with all its fullness." So how come we haven't taken advantage of it? We suspect that there are two reasons for this anomaly:

We are too easily satisfied. To paraphrase C.S. Lewis, most Christians are content to play in the mud puddles of their own backyards when Christ wants to take us on a vacation to the beach. That is sad, but even sadder is the fact that we don't realize what we are missing. As Tony Campolo says:

> Most people are born and years later die without really having lived at all…. [They] never reflect with any intensive awareness on any part of their lives. They eat and sleep, they work and reproduce, and they study and forget. They play it safe and tiptoe through life with no aspiration other than to arrive at death safely.

Don't let this happen to you! Don't settle for making mud pies when you could be bodysurfing. Live life to the extreme instead of tiptoeing your years away.

We have "analysis paralysis." Some of us can't get out of our rut because we can't decide what to do. We are afraid to live life to the extreme because we aren't sure that we want to do what we have to do to get there. We want the reward but not the risk. We want the excitement but at no expense. We want the euphoria without the effort. So, we keep thinking about it—without actually *doing* anything about it—until the coffin is nailed shut.

> Thinking without action is a lot like aiming without shooting. Seeing the target doesn't do you any good if you are never going to hit it.

Don't let this happen to you. Snap out of it. You have been thinking long enough; now is the time to spring into action.

Now, if you are reading this book, congratulate yourself. That fact alone shows that you are not content to settle for less than God's exciting best. And it also indicates that you are ready to move from *analysis* into *action*.

Extreme Regime

Maybe you are anxious to experience "life with all its fullness" but don't know how to get started. With all the advice that bombards you from every direction, who could blame you for being a little disoriented?

- Oprah is telling you to find the essence of life by looking to your inner self.
- Richard Simmons says that you can't find the *inner you* until you shed that outer flab.
- Get-rich-quick infomercials proclaim that you will experience real life to the extreme only after you achieve millionaire status from buying real estate foreclosures. (Other infomercials suggest you'll find real life in that rotisserie oven, or in that hair-in-a-can for male pattern baldness.)
- PBS is always good for a televised lecture by someone who encourages you to get more out of life (but the shows keep being interrupted by those annoying pledge drives).
- Car manufacturers would like you to believe that true excitement comes only from driving their particular model. (We've noticed that the commercials usually show a car zipping along the winding coastal highway at speeds over one hundred miles per hour. We agree that there is a degree of extreme excitement that comes with being a NASCAR driver, but we're interested in finding exhilaration that isn't necessarily life-threatening.)
- Even the beer commercials are telling you to "go for the gusto."

Forget all of the psychobabble. Don't order the get-rich-quick seminar tapes; and don't trade in your reliable sedan for that Dodge Viper. Remember, Jesus said *he* could give "life in all its fullness." You've got everything you need for an extreme life in your relationship with God. He can give you more life than you could even imagine.

But just knowing that God is the source of an extreme life doesn't solve your problem. You still need to know how to obtain it. You're savvy enough to realize that the secret is found somewhere in the Bible, but there are so many verses that it can be a bit confusing (not to mention those passages in Song of Solomon that are a bit distracting). But fret not. In the next eleven chapters we'll assist you in making sense of all of it. We'll help you discover some biblical principles for identifying and implementing God's extreme plan for your life.

Before we get to the specifics of making choices in your life that will give you the fullness that Jesus promised, there are two preparatory steps that you can begin to take. Each one is a necessary component to enjoying life to the fullest.

Step #1: Get Your Relationship Ready

God is anxious to guide you in the process of making choices that produce an extreme life. Some of his principles are available to everyone (or at least anyone who reads the Book of Proverbs). But much of his guidance is very personal and comes only in the context of a close one-to-one relationship. You'll have difficulty sensing God's divine guidance and direction if you are just casually acquainted with him.

If you are serious about learning God's will for your life, then you must begin by being serious about your relationship with him. Here are a few questions to help you assess the quality of your relationship with God:

Have you been reborn into God's family? This is a threshold question. You can't expect to receive God's blessings of a full life unless you are part of his family. Being religious is not enough; you must actually experience rebirth.

A religious leader named Nicodemus—who was looking for an extreme life—came to Jesus. He had been watching Jesus from afar, and he knew that Jesus was somehow connected to God because the supernatural element of Christ's life was obvious. Their interchange went like this:

> *"Teacher," he said, "we all know that God has sent you to teach us. Your miraculous signs are proof enough that God is with you."*
>
> *Jesus replied, "I assure you, unless you are born again, you can never see the Kingdom of God."*
>
> JOHN 3:2-3

As the conversation progressed, Jesus told Nicodemus God's overall plan for the human race. You probably recognize the explanation as John 3:16:

> *For God so loved the world that he gave his only Son, so that everyone who believes in him will not perish but have eternal life.*

Nicodemus was thrown a bit by Christ's reference to rebirth. Jesus explained that those who trust and believe in God receive the Holy Spirit, who produces new life in them. If you want to have an exciting, extreme life in which you experience the supernatural, then you must begin by being reborn into God's family.

Are you responsive to God's presence? There is a difference between just being in God's family and actually wanting to be in his presence. Think back a few years to when you were a teenager. You were in your parents' family, but you might not have enjoyed being in their presence. Remember those rebellious teenage years spent in your bedroom with the door locked?

As children of God, we often act like rebellious teenagers. We are part of God's family, but we don't really enjoy his presence. We would rather be off doing our own thing and going our own way. With that attitude, we shouldn't be surprised if life doesn't seem very fulfilling. Our lives will become extreme as we begin to realize the significance of what Christ promised:

> *And be sure of this: I am with you always, even to the end of the age.*
> MATTHEW 28:20

Your life will begin to change drastically when you realize that Christ is right there beside you.

Do you rely upon God's Word? If you want to know God's will for your life, then you must know God. And if you want to know God, then you have to know God's Word. This is a plain and simple fact. God uses his Word, the Bible, to teach us about himself. He also uses it to teach us about ourselves.

If you are sincerely interested in learning God's plan for your life, then you will become serious about reading his Word. Think of the Bible as God's personal message to you about yourself. His plans for you are laid out in the Bible:

> *All Scripture is inspired by God and is useful to teach us what is true and to make us realize what is wrong in our lives. It straightens us out and teaches us to do what is right. It is God's way of preparing us in every way, fully equipped for every good thing God wants us to do.*
> 2 TIMOTHY 3:16-17

Do you reflect God's love to others? As we will explain in the coming chapters, a key to knowing God's will for your life involves knowing the heart and mind of God. (That is *extreme* in itself—that we can know the intimate thoughts of the Creator of the Universe.) The Bible gives an easy way to determine whether or not you know God:

Anyone who loves is born of God and knows God. But anyone who does not love does not know God—for God is love.

1 JOHN 4:7-8

Love is one of the inescapable, unavoidable, and undeniable aspects of God. We all enjoy the benefits of being recipients of his love. For that reason, you might find it easy to love God. But if we truly belong to him, then he asks us to do something that might be a little more difficult: He wants us to love others.

Actually, loving others isn't all that difficult when you are filled with the love of Christ. It may be awkward at first, but kindness and thoughtfulness will begin to come naturally as you begin to give God control of your life. Your love for others will be evidence that you love God. As Jesus said:

Your love for one another will prove to the world that you are my disciples.

JOHN 13:35

Are you reaching out to God's world? Don't panic. We aren't going to tell you that giving your life to God automatically means packing up and becoming a missionary in Africa. (He might lead you there on a short-term opportunity, like he did our editor, but if that's his plan he'll put the desire in your heart first!)

At the same time, the Bible does make it clear that we should bring God into our network of family, friends, and associates. Sharing the good news about Christ doesn't always involve a pulpit or a pith helmet. It is as natural as telling someone about the great things that are happening in your life:

Go home to your friends, and tell them what wonderful things the Lord has done for you and how merciful he has been.

MARK 5:19

Step #2: Get Intentional

Many people miss out on God's exciting plans for their lives because they expect God to do all of the work. They sit around passively and do little more than vegetate. We speak from a degree of experience in this regard (as the indentations on our La-Z-Boy recliners will attest). But we can also tell you from personal experience that life gets pretty exciting when you become intentional about pursuing God's plan.

The apostle Paul knew all about living life to the extreme in the pursuit of following God's plan. If you don't believe so, read this autobiographical account of the adventures of his life:

They say they serve Christ? I know I sound like a madman, but I have served him far more! I have worked harder, been put in jail more often, been whipped times without number, and faced death again and again. Five different times the Jews gave me thirty-nine lashes. Three times I was beaten with rods. Once I was stoned. Three times I was shipwrecked. Once I spent a whole night and a day adrift at sea. I have traveled many weary miles. I have faced danger from flooded rivers and from robbers. I have faced danger from my own people, the Jews, as well as from the Gentiles. I have faced danger in the cities, in the deserts, and on the stormy seas. And I have faced danger from men who claim to be Christians but are not. I have lived with weariness and pain and sleepless nights. Often I have been hungry and thirsty and have gone without food. Often I have shivered with cold, without enough clothing to keep me warm.

2 CORINTHIANS 11:23-27

Are you still with us? We know we took a risk by using Paul as an example of an extreme life. Shipwrecks, assassination attempts, and imprisonment probably weren't what you had in mind when you started reading this book. Your interest in following God's will probably stops short of death threats.

The interesting thing about Paul's life is that all of these catastrophes did not deter him from pursuing God. He stayed intensely focused. And that is the advice that he gives to other Christians. He encourages us to pursue God deliberately and intentionally rather than passively. Look at the emphasis he places on intensity in these passages from his letters (we have highlighted a few words for your reading convenience):

- *No, dear brothers and sisters, I am still not all I should be, **but I am focusing all my energies** on this one thing: Forgetting the past and looking forward to what lies ahead, **I strain** to reach the end of the race and receive the prize for which God, through Christ Jesus, is calling us up to heaven.*

  PHILIPPIANS 3:13-14

- *So everywhere we go, we tell everyone about Christ. We **warn them and teach them** with all the wisdom God has given us, for we want to present them to God, perfect in their relationship to Christ. **I work very hard at this**, as I depend on Christ's mighty power that works within me.*

  COLOSSIANS 1:28-29

- *Remember that in a race everyone runs, but only one person gets the prize. **You also must run in such a way that you will win.** All athletes practice strict self-control. They do it to win a prize that will fade away, but we do it for an eternal prize. So **I run straight to the goal with purpose in every step.** I am not like a boxer who misses his punches. **I discipline my body like an athlete, training it to do what it should.***

  1 CORINTHIANS 9:24-27

The apostle Paul experienced an exhilarating life in all respects—emotionally, physically, and spiritually—because he was deliberate and intentional about pursuing God's plan. "Life in all its fullness" is also available to you, but you, too, must be intentional in your pursuit of God's will for your life.

Are You Ready for the Extreme?

This book is all about making choices that make a difference. We aren't talking about mundane choices between breakfast cereals or even the selection of your next new car. This book is about making choices that allow you to experience life to the extreme. In our humble (but correct) opinion, there is nothing more extreme than being in a personal relationship with God Almighty. In Chapter 2, we explore that incredible experience by examining the nature of God and how much he cares for you.

Who Is God and
What Does He Want From Me?

God is a personal Father who cares, not a God who
merely wound up the world with a key and then went
away to let it run by itself.

—*Spirit* magazine

Everybody has an opinion about God. Some people see him as a malevolent ogre (like the giant in *Jack and the Beanstalk*) who sits in heaven, thinking of ways to make life miserable for us lowly humans. One mistake and—BAM!—you're doing eternal time in the lake of fire, with all that gnashing and wailing and clanking chains.

Other people see God as a benevolent grandfather, kindly and forgiving like a superhuman Santa Claus. As long as you're more nice than naughty when you die—WHOOSH!—St. Peter will throw open the Pearly Gates and hand you a set of wings and a harp.

Both descriptions are ridiculous, of course. They're like something out of a bad movie or a silly cartoon. But a lot of people haven't thought much past these two extremes. How about you? How do you see God? What do you think about him? Does it all boil down to the simple prayer you learned as a kid: "God is great, God is good, let us thank him for our food"?

Why Do You Think About God?

Before we look at *what* you think about God, it's important to know *why* you think about God. Have you ever thought about that before? Why is it that every person who has ever lived—regardless of culture, language, location, and religious preference—has thought about God? Either we think about ways to please God, or we think about ways to avoid God. Either way, we think about him.

The answer is really quite simple: We have no choice.

When God created people, he installed a "God memory chip" that prompts us to think about him. Here's how the Bible explains this:

> *For the truth about God is known ... instinctively. God has put this knowledge in their hearts. From the time the world was created, people have seen the earth and sky and all that God made. They can clearly see his invisible qualities—his eternal power and divine nature. So they have no excuse whatsoever for not knowing God.*
>
> ROMANS 1:19-20

"What does all of this have to do with living life to the extreme?" you might ask. Good question. You bought this book (or someone gave it to you) to help you make good choices and find God's will for your life. You don't want to read a boring book about philosophy or theology.

We agree. The last thing we want to do is bore you. But we do want to challenge you. We want to help you think this stuff through for one very important reason that has everything to do with living your life to the extreme:

What you think about God
determines who you are
and how you live.

To prove our point, let's look at two possible scenarios for your life based on what you think about God. Notice how the outcome of your thinking dramatically impacts who you are and how you live your life.

Scenario #1:

You believe that God exists, and you want to live your life to please him. This scenario has the following implications:

- You believe that God created the universe and everything in it, including you.
- You believe you are one of God's special creations, and that your life is important and significant to him. You know that God loves you.
- Although you don't know exactly what it is, you believe that God has a plan for you.
- You are anxious to find out what that plan is.
- What you do has significance because it either fits into God's plan or it doesn't.
- The stuff that fits into God's plan is a lot better than the stuff that doesn't.
- There is an eternal, spiritual aspect to your life. Your physical death isn't the end of you.

Scenario #2:

You deny that God exists, or you believe he exists but you don't think he cares much about what you do, so you don't live your life to please him. This scenario also has some implications:

- The universe in which you live pretty much came from nothing, or God got it started like a wind-up toy and left it to run all by itself.
- Since God doesn't exist or doesn't care, there's no master plan for the world or for you.
- It's up to you to make your own way in this world and find your own significance.
- You can live how you want because no one is out there "judging" you.
- There's no spiritual or eternal dimension to your life, so when you die, that's it. Game over.

If you fall into Scenario #1, congratulations, but don't get smug. You may know the truth, but not everyone sees it that way. Many people who live their lives according to Scenario #2 think they are living life to the extreme, even if they aren't living with God's abundant fulfillment.

If you put yourself under Scenario #2, you're not a bad person. Hey, you've got plenty of company, including a lot of high achievers who have accomplished a lot of good in this world. On the other hand, what if you've miscalculated? What if, like the Russian cosmonaut who "disproved" God's existence by reporting that he had not seen heaven while in orbit, you are simply missing what's right in front of you?

But if God exists—and we know he does—it should make a difference in how you live.

The Big Deal About God

Many years ago a man named J.B. Phillips wrote a book called *Your God Is Too Small.* The premise is that we underestimate everything about God—his power, his personality, his mind, his vastness, and his involvement in our world. Even those of us in Scenario #1 think too little of God. It's as if we keep God in a box and take him out on Sundays and special occasions.

What a mistake! If we're ever going to get to know God, we need to take God out of our puny mental containers and see him as he is—the Creator and Master of the Universe.

If the President of the United States were to walk in on you right now, you would probably get pretty excited (even if you didn't vote for him). After all, this is the leader of the most powerful nation on earth. He's the number-one guy in the number-one country in the world. He deserves your respect.

Well, if the President could get that kind of reaction out of you, what about God? He's not in charge of the universe because a bunch of people got together and voted him in as Supreme Being. God is above everything and over everything because he made everything. He has always existed and he always will exist. Like the Wizard of Oz, God could have hidden himself in a celestial room somewhere, using a lot of smoke and thunder and occasionally giving us cryptic commands. But that's not God. True, there are a lot of things about God we can't possibly understand, but there is plenty of stuff we can know, thanks to the Bible.

God Has Given Us a Message

The Bible is the most unique and compelling book in the world because God is the author. The Bible is God's revelation of himself to people. It tells the story of God, and it delivers the message of God. Because God inspired (literally, "breathed into") forty different men to write down his words and his message, you don't have to wonder about God. You can *know* about God, and you can know what God expects of you.

You accepted what we said as the very word of God—which, of course, it was. And this word continues to work in you who believe.

1 THESSALONIANS 2:13

When you think about God and the Bible, you could conclude that the two form a kind of circular argument that goes something like this: *You believe in God, who wrote the Bible, so you believe in the Bible because God wrote it.* And you know what? You would be right—except for one thing. God exists apart from the Bible, but the Bible wouldn't exist without God. Remember, God wrote the Bible, not the other way around. That's why there are things about the Bible that you can't explain apart from God. Josh McDowell explains that only God could have created a book that:

- *Has been transmitted accurately from the time it was originally written.* No other ancient book can match the Bible's accuracy and reliability.
- *Is correct when it deals with historical people and events.* The Bible contains real people and real events that are proven correct when measured against objective history.
- *Contains no scientific absurdities.* The Bible isn't a scientific manual, and it doesn't use scientific terms, but its descriptions of how the world came to be and how it works are completely consistent with modern scientific data.
- *Remains true and relevant to all people for all time.* The Bible hasn't become dated or outmoded. It speaks as powerfully to us today as it did to people thousands of years ago.

The Bible is the only book of its kind and the only "holy" book with this kind of track record, and we haven't even talked about the 100 percent accuracy of the Bible prophecies. The Bible contains approximately 2,500 prophecies, and 2,000 have been fulfilled to the letter to date (they can be verified historically). World-renowned astrophysicist Dr. Hugh Ross estimates that the probability of any one of the prophecies coming true is less than one in ten. The chance that all 2,000 prophecies could have been fulfilled by chance without error is less than one in 10 to the 2000th power, which by mathematical standards is considered an impossibility. Only God can accomplish the impossible, and he did it through the Bible.

What Does the Bible Say About God?

Knowing that the Bible is accurate and reliable is incredibly important, because the Bible tells us a great deal about God and the world he made. By reading the Bible we can find out what God did in the beginning and what God is doing now. As we look at each of these, we can also discover what the Bible says about who God is.

What God Did in the Beginning

In the beginning God created the heavens and the earth.

GENESIS 1:1

We're all familiar with that verse, and there's a reason why it's the first verse in the Bible. It explains very clearly that God is the First Cause of the universe. Science has always recognized the law of cause and effect, which means that you can't have an effect without cause. Until recently, however, scientists didn't apply the law of cause and effect to the beginning of the universe. The prevailing scientific view was that the universe is eternal, with no beginning. Today all that has changed, thanks to some dramatic scientific evidence uncovered at the end of the 20th century (you remember the 20th century, don't you?).

Sophisticated scientific instruments, like the Cosmic Background Explorer, have demonstrated that there was a point in time when the universe exploded into being out of nothing (it's called the big bang). Science isn't ready yet to tell us what caused that first big bang, but most scientists will agree that the beginning of the universe had a cause. Astronomer Robert Jastrow makes this observation:

> I am fascinated by the implications in some of the scientific developments of recent years. The essence of these developments is that the Universe had, in some sense, a beginning. It began at a certain moment in time, and under circumstances that seem to make it impossible—not just now, but ever—to find out what force or forces brought the world into being at that moment.[1]

What Jastrow is saying is that we know there was a beginning, and we know that some force caused the beginning, but we can't prove what that force was. He even speculates that the Bible could be right in telling us that God was the "Prime Mover."

Scientists like Dr. Jastrow may not be able to explain who or what the Prime Mover is, but they know that this something or Someone would have to be transcendent, existing apart from and independent of humanity, nature, and the universe. Only God fits that requirement. *Only God could have created the universe and everything in it because only God is transcendent.*

Here are some other things we know about God from his role as the First Cause of the universe:

- *God is **omnipotent*** (all-powerful). The amount of energy unleashed in the big bang is unimaginable, yet all God had to do was say the word. The Bible says it this way: "By faith we understand that the entire universe was formed at God's command" (Hebrews 11:3). Imagine the power! Imagine, like the prophet Jeremiah, what this means for us.

O Sovereign LORD! You have made the heavens and earth by your great power. Nothing is too hard for you!

JEREMIAH 32:17

As you're going to see throughout this book, God's sovereignty—his absolute power—created the universe, but God's power is also available to you personally.

- *God is **omniscient*** (all-knowing). The universe is incredibly complex and intricate, from the farthest realms of space to the nearly invisible world of subatomic particles. The more science learns about the universe and how it works, the more scientists believe that the universe didn't assemble itself. It was carefully and amazingly designed.

More and more scientists (including those in Scenario #2) are talking about an "intelligent design," even if they don't talk about God. That's OK. As the evidence for design continues to pour in from virtually every scientific discipline, there will be no denying that the intelligent designer is God.

Of course, the Bible has already told us that only God has the knowledge and understanding to create the universe: "His understanding is beyond comprehension" (Psalm 147:5). God knows everything about the universe because he created the universe. And he knows everything about you because he created you.

> *O LORD, you have examined my heart and know everything about me.*
>
> PSALM 139:1

- *God is **omnipresent*** (he's everywhere at once). God is a Spirit, and he is bigger than the universe. The Bible says, "Nothing in all creation can hide from him" (Hebrews 4:13), and that applies to you as well. On the negative side, you can never run from God. On the positive side, he will always be with you wherever you go. Now, that's extreme!

> *I can never escape from your spirit! I can never get away from your presence!*
>
> PSALM 139:7

- *God is **eternal*** (timeless). God exists apart from the universe, and he exists beyond the universe. This applies to time as well as space. The Bible says, "You are God, without beginning or end" (Psalm 90:2). What does this mean to you? It means that when your life is over, it won't be over. God has plans for you that extend beyond your physical life on earth.

What God Is Doing Now

In the next chapter we're going to get into some fairly complex issues about God and his involvement in the world (including your life). We're going to talk about a little thing called *providence*, which has nothing to do with the capital of Rhode Island. The word *providence* is used to describe God's ongoing relationship with his creation.

> *He sustains the universe by the mighty power of his command.*
>
> HEBREWS 1:3

God didn't just create the universe, then step back and let everything happen on its own (this philosophy is called *deism*). The psalmist David observed that "the earth is full of your creatures" (Psalm 104:24), who would die if God took away their breath (see Psalm 104:29). God is actively involved in preserving the universe and everything in it, down to the minutest detail. God remains involved so that all things (from plants to humans) fulfill the purposes for which he created them. That is providence. It is also the basis for science, for technology, for life itself. Theologian Wayne Grudem observes:

> God, in preserving all things, also causes them to maintain the properties with which he created them. God preserves water in such a way that it continues to act like water. He causes grass to continue to act like grass, with all its distinctive characteristics. He causes the paper on which this sentence is written to continue to act like paper so that it does not spontaneously dissolve into water and float away or change into a living thing and begin to grow!

Just as God's providence gives us a basis for science and technology, it also tells us something about who God is:

- God is *immutable* (unchangeable). "I am the LORD, and I do not change," says God (Malachi 3:6). We don't doubt that the sun will come up tomorrow, and we can count on God to act as he always has. This should give you confidence as you think about your life.

- God is *love*. Only a God of love would care so much for his creation. Think of what that means to you personally. Here's how Jesus put it:

And if God cares so wonderfully for flowers that are here today and gone tomorrow, won't he more surely care for you?

MATTHEW 6:30

How Do You Fit Into All of This?

Thinking about the universe and how it got here and how huge and complex it is and how it all works should stretch your brain and give you an entirely new appreciation for God. But how does all of this make you feel about you? Do you feel that you are an important part of the universe or an insignificant speck?

It's perfectly natural to think about the vastness of the universe and wonder why God even bothers with us humans. The psalmist David put it this way:

When I look at the night sky and see the work of your fingers—the moon and the stars you have set in place—what are mortals that you should think of us, mere humans that you should care for us?

PSALM 8:3-4

Why does God care about us mortals? What's so special about us that God knows us down to the number of hairs on our heads? Well, there's one very big reason: we are created in the image of God. When you read the account of Creation in Genesis 1, you see a particular order for how things came into existence (an order that science agrees with, by the way). First came light, followed by atmosphere, sea, land, plants and creatures. Then God created his crowning achievement—humankind. In many ways this new kind of created being resembled some of the creatures God made. But in one very big way, human beings were completely unique and set apart from everything else in creation.

> *God created people in his own image; God patterned them after himself; male and female he created them.*
>
> GENESIS 1:27

Often people in Scenario #2 will tell you that you are little more than a naked ape. Don't believe it! You are a human being made in God's image. You have God's divine imprint. You and you alone—

- Can communicate with God
- Have the responsibility to manage the earth's resources
- Are responsible to obey God
- Have a spiritual nature

We're going to explore these spiritual qualities in more detail in the next few chapters, but we want to close this chapter by posing a very important question.

Why Are You Here?

There are a lot of important questions you will ponder in your lifetime:

- Should vegetarians eat animal crackers?
- Why doesn't glue stick to the inside of a bottle?
- What's another word for *synonym*?

Of all these questions, there is none more important than this: *Why am I here?* (Sometimes people ask this in other ways, such as, *What is my purpose in life?*)

How would you answer that question? If you're waiting to answer until you figure out what you want to do with your life, forget it. You'll never come up with a definite answer because few people ever get to the point where they definitely know what they want to do (we sure haven't).

There's a much better way to answer the question because the Bible has already told you. Don't worry, this isn't going to lock you into something you don't want to do. It's simply going to explain why God created you in the first place, which should give you a pretty good handle on why you're here. Are you ready? Here it is (drum roll, please):

God created you for his own glory. That's why you're here.

If you don't believe us, read what God himself said:

All who claim me as their God will come, for I have made them for my glory. It was I who created them.

ISAIAH 43:7

Talk about having significance! God didn't create you because he was lonely or bored. He created you for his own glory. Wayne Grudem writes:

This is the final definition of genuine importance or significance to our lives: If we are truly important to God for all eternity, then what greater measure of importance or significance could we want? That's why the apostle Paul wrote: "Whatever you eat or drink or whatever you do, you must do all for the glory of God" (1 Corinthians 10:31).[2]

Talk about living life to the extreme! You don't have to wonder if the person you are and the things you do matter to God. You don't have to worry that you're going to end up in a dead-end career. God created you so you could enjoy his blessings and benefits throughout your life and give him all the credit he deserves. As the Bible says:

No eye has seen, no ear has heard, and no mind has imagined what God has prepared for those who love him.

This is where it really gets good (and you've only read two chapters). Even though it seems hard to understand, God has plans for you that are beyond your imagination. In the next chapter we're going to look at how God is involved in your life (whether you realize it or not).

CHAPTER 3

Discovering God's Plan
for Your Life

> "Would you tell me, please, which way I ought to go from here?"
>
> "That depends a good deal on where you want to get to," said the Cat.
>
> "I don't much care where—" said Alice.
>
> "Then it doesn't matter which way you go," said the Cat.
>
> —Lewis Carroll, *Alice in Wonderland*

Have you ever stopped to wonder how involved God wants to be in the day-to-day circumstances of your life? Where does God's control stop and your personal freedom begin?

- Has he mapped out your career path from burger-flipper to CEO?
- Will he send you on a wild search for the only person in the universe created to be your spouse? (And just for laughs, will he or she be born in Outer Mongolia in the year 2025?)
- Does it matter to him if you drink Pepsi or Coke?

And then there's the big picture to consider. Doesn't the war in Bosnia merit a little more of his attention than your stubbed toe? Do you even want God to think about your parking space when famine is killing so many children in Africa? Before you can come to grips with decision making in your own life, you'll need to understand God's role in the circumstances of your life.

People often conceptualize the interplay between God and humanity into one of several basic scenarios. We won't bore you with the theological or philosophical terminology. We think you'll find our labels a little more memorable:

The Robot Theory: This concept has us responding to God's commands like a remote-controlled robot. From all outward indications, it would appear that we are making our own decisions. But up in heaven, God is directing us through the circumstances of life by the simple movement of his celestial joystick. He completely programs what we do, and we don't even realize it.*

The Jiminy Cricket Theory: God is like an extraterrestrial Jiminy Cricket. You have complete freedom to go your own way and do your own thing, but God is your cosmic conscience. He watches over you and lays a heap of celestial guilt on you when you get out of line. (Fortunately, you have built up a tolerance to guilt after years of nagging from your mother, so God's guilt doesn't really cramp your style.)

The Teenager Theory: God is like a father, and we are his children. But we aren't little toddler children who are kept in the playpen. We are like teenagers. We can pretty much do whatever we like, and there isn't much our father can do to stop us. Some of us are rebellious and break curfew. We

---

* The Robot Theory is just an updated version of the Ventriloquist Theory, which made God the ventriloquist and you his dummy. (The dummy can't do anything by itself; the ventriloquist brings it to life and puts words in its mouth. When the ventriloquist is finished, the dummy gets put in a box.) The technological developments in the field of robotics and the demise of television variety shows precipitated the change in terminology.

know that there may be some punishment involved when we eventually get caught, but we will worry about that when it happens. Others are compliant and follow the rules. We expect to be rewarded for our good behavior (like by an increase in our allowance).

The Harlem Globetrotters Theory: Life is a game; we are the players, but God is the referee. The referee controls the game—changing the rules if he has to—to make sure that the Globetrotters win and the Washington Generals lose. If you are the referee's favorite, you can do whatever you want and the rules don't apply to you. If you are a Washington General, then it doesn't matter how great an athlete you are. Every call is going against you.

The Ant Farm Theory: The world is like God's ant farm, and we are the little critters inside. God just sets the world in place and watches us go about our business of burrowing tunnels and being busy. He never interferes with us; he just watches. We are free to do whatever we want (and we live our entire lives without realizing that we are sandwiched between glass barriers that define our reality).

As we will discuss, none of these theories have correctly captured the interplay between God's control and your choice that is described in the Bible. None of them allow for God to be in charge while still allowing you to exercise your free will.

The Bible describes an interesting, dynamic interaction between God's will and your choices. God is definitely in charge (sovereign), but you have the ability to make decisions and choices. Said another way:

Your freedom is subject to God's control.

There are two aspects to God's sovereignty: his position (no one outranks him) and his power. Everyone else (including Satan) has power only as permitted by God.

As the Sovereign Being, God could choose to be a dictator, but he hasn't done so. Conversely, he could choose to relinquish all of his power, but he hasn't done that either. Instead, he has allowed us free will. As a result, he chooses to let certain things happen according to natural laws that he set in place.

In the entire universe, not a single molecule is outside the scope of God's sovereignty. (If that happened, then God wouldn't be sovereign.) This thought should be quite comforting to you because it means that God is truly in charge of the universe. And if he has the universe under control, then he has you covered. Every aspect of life operates under the auspices of his control:

- Your day-to-day plans (see James 4:13-15);
- The existence and functioning of creation (see Revelation 4:11);
- The decisions of political leaders (see Proverbs 21:1); and
- The problems that besiege you (see 1 Peter 3:17).

Of course, the fact that God is sovereign doesn't mean that he dictates how everything will happen. He exercises his sovereignty in a manner that allows things to happen in their own course. At the same time, nothing happens without his permission. He chooses to allow some things to happen. Don't miss the significance of this principle:

**Nothing that happens to us
catches God by surprise;
and nothing happens to us that
God has not specifically allowed.**

Although there might be times in your life when you think that events are spinning out of control, God is in charge of every circumstance and situation. Everything operates according to his sovereign plan:

All things happen just as he decided long ago.

EPHESIANS 1:11

But What About the Bad Stuff That Happens?

If God permitted only the good and prohibited the bad, then you wouldn't be allowed to exercise your free will. But God is not defeated or even discouraged by the bad things that happen in the world. Because God is sovereign, he can arrange the circumstances to bring a good result out of a bad situation:

And we know that God causes everything to work together for the good of those who love God and are called according to his purpose for them.
ROMANS 8:28

Not everything that happens in the world is good, but God can use anything that happens to produce a good result. (The best example of this principle is the crucifixion of Jesus Christ.) We may not be able to see how this is possible when something bad is happening to us. That's where it becomes a matter of *trust*.

We have a friend who told us the story of her sister Chris, who had cancer when she was a little girl. After several operations and treatments, Chris had to have her leg removed to give her the best chance of living a normal life again. The night before it happened, our friend couldn't sleep. She was angry with God. After all, hadn't her entire church prayed for her sister's healing? Didn't God know that Chris had a lot of athletic ability, that she loved to ski and cheerlead and horseback ride? Why did Chris have to lose her leg?

Our friend's mother wasn't sleeping either, and she came and sat beside her daughter. Wisely, she didn't put down her daughter's feelings. Instead, she quietly said, "God does know all those things. He made her with all that energy and determination. He knew she'd need it, to be able to face this battle she is in right now."

As human beings, we have certain limitations. We cannot look into the future or change the past. Unlike God, we are not omniscient or omnipresent. And so, we must cling to what we know to be true about God: He knows what we need in order to become who he wants us to be.

Although we may not understand (or even like) what is happening, we can rest in the assurance that God knows what he is doing and has everything under control.

God's Providence, Your Protection

Just because God is sovereign, he isn't required to be an active participant in the events of your life. He could have all events under control but just sit back and watch while things happen. (Remember the Ant Farm Theory?) But God isn't like that. He is totally involved in what happens in your life. Theologians refer to God's participation as *providence*.

Creation was God's act of forming the universe. Providence is his continuing relationship to it.

There are at least two distinct aspects to God's providence:

He holds creation together. God's continued involvement (his providence) preserves the existence of creation. Without that continued involvement, the universe would cease to exist.

> *Everything has been created through him and for him. He existed before everything else began, and he holds all creation together.*
>
> COLOSSIANS 1:16-17

He guides and directs circumstances to fulfill his purposes. God's affirmative and proactive involvement in the course of events is sometimes referred to as God's *governing* activity. In his treatise *Christian Theology,* Professor Millard J. Erickson explains the extent of God's governing activity.

- God asserts control over nature (see Psalm 135:5-7) and animals (see Psalm 104:21-29);
- God influences human history and the destiny of nations (see Daniel 4:24-25) and the lives of individual persons (1 Samuel 2:6-7);

- God specially equips believers with supernatural spiritual gifts (see Romans 12:3-6);
- God is actually involved in events that might otherwise appear to be accidental occurrences of life (see Jonah 1:7); and
- God even uses the sinful actions of humans to accomplish his purposes (see Acts 2:23).

Preservation is important (you wouldn't be here without it). But this book is all about making choices, and the aspect of God's governing impacts the daily dynamics of decision making for your life.

God's providence—his governing activity—even extends to our own personal salvation. That's right! God was instrumental in bringing you to the point of salvation.

For God knew his people in advance, and he chose them to become like his Son, so that his Son would be the firstborn, with many brothers and sisters. And having chosen them, he called them to come to him. And he gave them right standing with himself, and he promised them his glory.

ROMANS 8:29-30

So What's Left for You to Choose?

People have been debating the nature of free will since—well, since people have been debating. The reason is that free will goes to the heart of human nature.

Some people think that *free will* is a basic human right—like voting and cable. They ask, "Why would God interfere with your ability to make choices if he gave you the ability to choose?"

Others think *free will* is an oxymoron—like *honest lawyer* or *jumbo shrimp*. They ask, "How can the will be free as long as God is sovereign?"

Still others think that we aren't even capable of choosing a holy God because of our sinful natures. (They cite Romans 3:11).

The truth is, there is much about this issue that we with our finite minds cannot hope to fully comprehend in this lifetime. (That's where the "trust" part kicks in again.) However, if we search the Scriptures, there are some things we know for sure. Here are two passages that give us a glimpse of God's plan for Christians who want to live "life in all its fullness"—life to the extreme! (Here and in later Bible texts, we have highlighted the points we are trying to emphasize.)

It is God who saved us and chose us to live a holy life. He did this not because we deserved it, but because that was his plan long before the world began.

2 TIMOTHY 1:9

Long ago, even before he made the world, God loved us and chose us in Christ to be holy and without fault in his eyes. His unchanging plan has always been to adopt us into his own family by bringing us to himself through Jesus Christ.

EPHESIANS 1:4-5

God's Mercy, Our Road to Freedom

Holy? Without fault? Was Paul kidding when he said that? After all, if we cannot even choose God for ourselves, if God must choose *us* before we can choose *him*, what hope do we have of ever becoming *holy*?

That's a good question—one that the apostle Paul, who was a great example of "extreme living," wrestled with, too:

I don't understand myself at all, for I really want to do what is right, but I don't do it. Instead, I do the very thing that I hate.... No matter which way I turn, I can't make myself do right. I want to, but I can't. When I want to do good, I don't.... Oh, what a miserable person I am! Who will free me from this life that is dominated by sin?

ROMANS 7:15,18-24

Satan has deceived us, and our free will is in bondage, but God calls us to break free by responding to Christ out of our own free will. We're under a spiritual death sentence, but God offers life instead.

> *Thank God! The answer is in Jesus Christ our Lord.... So now there is no condemnation for those who belong to Jesus Christ. For the power of the life-giving Spirit has freed you through Christ Jesus from the power of sin that leads to death.*
>
> ROMANS 7:25; 8:1-2

In case we missed it the first time, he reiterates this truth in the Book of Ephesians:

> *But God is so rich in mercy, and he loved us so very much, that even while we were dead because of our sins, he gave us life when he raised Christ from the dead.*
>
> EPHESIANS 2:4-5

The definition of *mercy* is "not getting what you deserve." We deserve death, because that's the penalty for going against God. But God sent Christ to die in our place, and then he raised Christ from the dead to give us life. That is pure mercy.

The definition of *grace* is "getting what you don't deserve." We don't deserve God's favor, but he gives it to us anyway because he loves us so very much. The ultimate grace gift is salvation, because there's nothing any of us can do to earn it. We don't deserve God's gift of life, but he gives it to us anyway. All we have to do is believe and accept it.

> *God saved you by his special favor when you believed. And you can't take credit for this; it is a gift from God. Salvation is not a reward for the good things we have done, so none of us can boast about it.*
>
> EPHESIANS 2:8-9

Able to Choose God

Something wonderful happens when we make the choice to follow God by believing in Jesus: God changes us into a new people. Before we accept God's free gift of salvation, we have no desire for God. We aren't even capable of choosing him. Once we respond to God, he changes our desire. For the first time in our lives we are able to choose God, and here's why:

What this means is that those who become Christians become new persons. They are not the same anymore, for the old life is gone. A new life has begun!

2 CORINTHIANS 5:17

This new life means that God gives us a desire to follow him and do what he says. He makes us aware that he has some incredible things in mind for us, which could be classified under the category of "God's will." That's what the next two chapters are all about: finding and doing God's will.

God's will can seem mysterious at times, but there's nothing to fear. To the contrary, we can live with the wonderful anticipation that God has some big plans in mind for us.

For we are God's masterpiece. He has created us anew in Christ Jesus, so that we can do the good things he planned for us long ago.

EPHESIANS 2:10

As we close this chapter, we'd like to leave you with an encouraging reminder of the reason we can be confident of finding and carrying out those plans:

And now, all glory to God, who is able to keep you from stumbling, and who will bring you into his glorious presence innocent of sin and with great joy. All glory to him, who alone is God our Savior, through Jesus Christ our Lord. Yes, glory, majesty, power, and authority belong to him, in the beginning, now, and forevermore. Amen.

JUDE 24-25

CHAPTER 4

Finding God's Will:
A Process of Discovery

I was going around in a circle
until God gave me a compass.

—Lynn Langley

Ever since you were a young child, you have been playing guessing games that are all variations on the "try and find me" theme. It started very simplistically, but the pattern has evolved in its complexity:

- As soon as you were a few months old, your mother began torturing you with "peek-a-boo." Putting her face about eight inches from yours, she covered her eyes with her hands and tried to make you believe that she had disappeared. How dumb did she think you were? You couldn't see her eyes, but so what? Her entire carcass—about twenty times the size of your body—was still hovering over you. You were amused by the fact that your mother thought she had tricked you with this disappearing act. You laughed that she was so easily deluded. Unfortunately, that sarcastic smile on your face only encouraged her to continue the annoying game.

- By the time you were five years old, the "peek-a-boo" torture had long since ended. (It came to an abrupt halt after you poked your finger in your mom's eye as she opened her hands.) But your life was still shrouded with "now you see it—now you don't" encounters. Remember when your grandpa would show you a piece of candy and then put his hands behind his back and make you guess which hand held the candy? Every time he'd pull the "old switcheroo"; no matter which hand you picked, you'd end up looking at nothing but an empty palm. After about five alternating picks, he'd finally let you win, and he handed you the candy and tousled your hair. (Of course, you didn't want to eat the candy after he had fondled it for several minutes. Even if it was M&Ms, it did melt in his hands, so you had sticky stuff in your hair after he tousled it.)

- The level of "try and find me" sophistication was cranked up a notch as you entered grade school and began to play hide 'n' seek with your older siblings. Somehow, they always managed to find you, but you were never successful in finding them. Only as an adult did you discover that they used the game as a way to ditch you. As you counted slowly to one hundred, they snuck out of the house to watch television with the neighbor kids. Their cruelty ended up costing you thousands of dollars for therapy to cure you from the fear of abandonment.

- As a teenager, you were a sucker for that game where a bean is placed under one of three cups, and then the cups are shuffled around, and you try to guess which one is covering the bean. It looked so easy, but you were always wrong. You should have learned that you weren't a good guesser. That lesson could have saved you a lot of money when you got to college and the game in the dormitory changed to three-card Monty at five bucks a pop.

But now you are an adult, and the guessing games have come to an end. Or have they? Don't you have that same, desperate "try and find me" feeling when you are guessing which stock to pick for your 401(k) investment?

Let's face it! Our past experiences have led us to believe that much of life is a guessing game. We approach every aspect of life with that mentality, whether we are participating in the office Super Bowl pool, buying a used car, signing up for a cellular calling plan, or choosing between either the Hollywood grapefruit diet or the all-protein, no-carbs diet plan. Whatever it is, we hope that we have picked the right one, but we know that we are just guessing.

God Doesn't Play Guessing Games

This guessing approach to life has subtly influenced our theology. We often think that determining God's will for our lives is like:

A Grandpa With Candy

God is like a heavenly grandfather who is holding his hands behind his back. In one of his hands is the perfect plan for our lives. In the other there's zilch. We've got to pick a hand. He isn't so sadistic as to pull the old switcheroo behind his back, but we run the risk that we might make the wrong choice and come up empty-handed. The anxiety between choosing the left hand or the right hand can be unbearable due to the consequences of a wrong guess.

Hide 'n' Seek

God has a plan for us, and we have to find it. He has hidden it somewhere, and we have to scurry around to find it. It is a celestial game of hide 'n' seek. If we find his will, then we win the game of life. If we don't find it, we end up being a big loser. We live our lives in a state of panic as we frantically search everywhere, even though we aren't sure what we're looking for.

The Bean-Under-the-Cup Game

Just when we think we have a clear vision of God's will, he keeps moving it around on us. We lose track of it. He is a master at sleight of hand in rearranging the circumstances of our lives to confuse and bewilder us. It gets to the point where we are so befuddled and disoriented that we simply have to guess at where we think his will has ended up.

If you conceptualize your search for God's will in any manner like this, you will forever be frustrated with the choices that confront you and worried that you'll guess incorrectly. But God doesn't want you to live with such feelings of frustration and anxiety. And he isn't interested in playing guessing games with you about something as important as his will.

Know What You're Looking For

Remember when you were playing "hide 'n' seek" but your older siblings ditched you? You were looking for something that wasn't there. Do you ever get the feeling that you are looking for God's will but he doesn't have one for you? Well, the Bible clearly states that God has a will for your life:

> *We ask God to give you a complete understanding of what he wants to do in your lives.*
>
> COLOSSIANS 1:9

> *Teach me to do your will, for you are my God.*
>
> PSALM 143:10

> *Anyone who wants to do the will of God will know whether my teaching is from God or is merely my own.*
>
> JOHN 7:17

> *This letter is from Paul, chosen by the will of God to be an apostle of Christ Jesus.*
>
> 1 CORINTHIANS 1:1

If you still aren't convinced that God has a plan and a will for your life, then maybe these statements from Jesus will change your mind.

My nourishment comes from doing the will of God, who sent me, and from finishing his work.

JOHN 4:34

For I have come down from heaven to do the will of God who sent me, not to do what I want.

JOHN 6:38

Christ was intent on following God's will. You probably want to do the same thing. That may be why you are working so hard to find God's will. But if God has a will for your life, and if you are looking for it, why is it so hard to find? Maybe you are right in the middle of it and don't realize it. Maybe you have been so anxious to receive a direct answer that you missed God's divine assistance.

God's Will: It's Mostly About Relationship

We suspect that you are anxious to know God's will for your life because you need answers to some important questions. Not the trivial "Wendy's or Burger King" or "boxers or briefs" type of choices. We mean life-impacting issues, such as:

Should I get more education? Your high-school diploma (and maybe even your college one) has been sitting in the attic awhile. Now what? Does God want you to devote a substantial sum of cash and time to getting an advanced degree or other training? Or should you simply hit the pavement and find a job?

Should I get married? If the answer is yes, then you've got the even bigger "To whom?" question to deal with.

Where should I live? You probably aren't worried about God's opinion on whether you choose between renting a condo downtown or an apartment in the suburbs. You want to know if God wants you to move across the country because your college roommate lives in Seattle and the possibilities seem intriguing.

What career should I choose? This question usually arises whenever you are dissatisfied with the one in which you currently find yourself.

How should I invest my money? You have always planned to quit working at age fifty, but you don't want to be so strapped for cash that you have to move back home with your parents when you do. You need to make some good long-range financial decisions right now.

Faced with such issues, you might be waiting for God to reveal his will with some specific answers—as specific as possible. So, you are praying hard and waiting for some type of divine revelation in which you will hear the voice of God provide you with responses like:

- "Get an MBA. Don't quit your job. Enroll in the part-time, night-school program. And don't forget to ask your employer to help subsidize the tuition costs."
- "Yes, you should get married, but not right now. You'll fall in love on July 17 of next year. I won't tell you the name of this person, but be looking for someone who is carrying a book written by Bruce & Stan (they are my favorite authors). You will date seriously for 43 weeks, and you will be engaged for 7 months. The colors of your wedding will be black and orange (trust me, it will work). Enjoy your honeymoon in Maui."
- "Forget Seattle. Stay in Nashville."
- "That chimney sweep franchise is a dead-end business. The careers for the future are biotech or solar power. Take your pick."
- "I told you not to buy stock in Pets.com, but you didn't listen to me. Maybe now you've learned your lesson. Stay out of cattle futures, and implement an investment strategy based on dollar cost averaging to acquire a diversified portfolio in large cap growth stocks balanced with municipal bonds."

Wouldn't it be great if God revealed his will that specifically? But that is not likely to happen. God's will isn't usually that specific.

If you are waiting for detailed answers from God to specific questions, you aren't likely to get them. But you already know this from personal experience, and that's why you think that you are forced to "guess" at God's will.

If you have had a difficult time determining God's will for your life, then you are reading the right book because we know what it is. Yes, that's right, even though we don't know you on a first-name basis (or a last-name basis either), we can announce with complete certainty God's will for your life. And we know that's what you are waiting to hear, so—without any further ado—can we have a drum roll, please?

It is God's will for your life that you become more and more like Christ each day.

We know you are a bit disappointed because our announcement doesn't give you any guidance about your career, your finances or your relationships. You were hoping for some specifics. Well, just wait. We are a few pages away from telling you how becoming more like Christ can help you with the choices in your life. But for now, let's focus on the biblical truth regarding God's will for your life. Here are some verses that plainly state God's will for your life and what he wants you to do:

- God wants you to be more like Christ, so at the outset it is God's will that you accept Christ as your Savior and believe in him:

*And **this is the will of God**, that I should not lose even one of all those he has given me, but that I should raise them to eternal life at the last day. For **it is my Father's will** that all who see his Son and believe in him should have eternal life.*

JOHN 6:39-40

- The process of being more like Christ doesn't stop with accepting him as your Savior. It includes living a holy lifestyle:

God wants you to be holy, so you should keep clear of all sexual sin. Then each of you will control your body and live in holiness and honor—not in lustful passion as the pagans do, in their ignorance of God and his ways.

1 THESSALONIANS 4:3-5

- Becoming more like Christ also involves maintaining a close, personal relationship with him that envelops your entire life:

*And now, Israel, **what does the LORD your God require of you?** He requires you to fear him, to live according to his will, to love and worship him with all your heart and soul, and to obey the LORD's commands and laws that I am giving you today.*

DEUTERONOMY 10:12-13

- Simply stated, as you become more like Christ, you will lead a moral, loving life that is in submission to God. That is exactly what God wants from you. That is his will for your life:

*O people, the Lord has already told you what is good, and **this is what he requires:** to do what is right, to love mercy, and to walk humbly with your God.*

MICAH 6:8

Help! I Need REAL Answers!

Perhaps you don't find these general "be like Christ" directives to be very helpful. You want some divine guidance with some difficult decisions you've got to make. You were hoping that God would give you guidance by revealing his will for your life with a little more specificity than just to love God "with all your heart and soul."

Although he may not always give you itemized responses to your specific questions, God will direct your thinking processes as you make your decisions. This is why it is his will for your life that you become more and more like Christ: so you will know how God thinks. Specifically—

- Becoming more like Christ allows you to reject the world's mentality and begin to consider your choices from God's perspective:

And so, dear brothers and sisters,... don't copy the behavior and customs of this world, but let God transform you into a new person by changing the way you think. Then you will know what God wants you to do, and you will know how good and pleasing and perfect his will really is.

ROMANS 12:1-2

- As you begin to know God more intimately, your conduct will change and the decisions you make will be ones that are within his plan:

We ask God to give you a complete understanding of what he wants to do in your lives, and we ask him to make you wise with spiritual wisdom. Then the way you live will always honor and please the Lord, and you will continually do good, kind things for others. All the while, you will learn to know God better and better.

COLOSSIANS 1:9-10

- As you experience God at work in your life, you will begin to trust him more. When you trust God, he will guide you in making your choices:

Trust in the Lord with all your heart; do not depend on your own understanding. Seek his will in all you do, and he will direct your paths.

PROVERBS 3:5-6

Are you beginning to see what these verses reveal about God's will for your life? It is not so much a specific person, or place, or time, or thing, or action. Instead, God's will is that you make decisions that are consistent with godliness.

**You don't have to worry about making
"the right decision"
as long as you are making
an "upright" decision.**

God's Will: More Like a Circle Than a Dot

In his book *Decision Making and the Will of God,* Dr. Garry Friesen explains that most people mistakenly think of God's will as a dot, one pinpoint of a specific answer. Under this misconception, people have to worry and fret about whether they have found the right dot. They worry that, if they miss it, then they are out of God's will.

In his book Dr. Friesen uses Scripture to explain that God's will is more like a large circle. The circle encompasses all moral and ethical and spiritual behavior that is consistent with God's character. He explains that decisions that are made within that circle are within God's will. You don't have to worry about picking a specific dot so long as you are within the circle.

God's Will: More About Guidance Than Guessing

Don't think about God's will in terms of specific responses. Instead, consider that God's will is all about maintaining an intimate relationship with him. If your heart and mind are constantly connected with God, then the things that are important to him will influence your decisions. This makes knowing God's will a matter of *spiritual guidance* rather than *human guesswork*.

So long as you are operating within the scope of God's character, you have freedom to make decisions without worrying that you have made the "wrong" choice. While this approach to God's will may seem more generalized than you would prefer, it actually applies to all areas of your life:

- It guides your aspirations:

So our aim is to please him always.

2 CORINTHIANS 5:9

- It guides your attitudes:

Your attitude should be the same that Christ Jesus had.

PHILIPPIANS 2:5

- It guides your actions:

Follow God's example in everything you do, because you are his dear children.... Make the most of every opportunity for doing good in these evil days. Don't act thoughtlessly, but try to understand what the Lord wants you to do.

EPHESIANS 5:1, 16-17

There is no guessing with God's will. It is a simple matter of conforming your life—your thoughts and actions—to be consistent with God's character. As that happens, then God will guide your decisions. He may not tell you specific answers, but you can make your choice in the confidence that he is guiding you:

He leads the humble in what is right, teaching them his way.

PSALM 25:9

The Lord says, "I will guide you along the best pathway for your life. I will advise you and watch over you."

PSALM 32:8

Follow Your Guide

The Bible doesn't use the word *guidance*, but it does refer to God as our guide. When you think about it, a guide is always better than guidance. In *The Fight*, author John White discusses God's will, and he uses an analogy to traffic to explain that a guide is better than mere guidance.

Suppose you were driving in heavy traffic in a strange city. (Let's use New York City as an example. It has heavy traffic, and it is very strange.) If you needed directions to the World Trade Center, someone could give you *guidance* by providing you with a long, detailed, and complicated set of directions. This might help, but you would be better off with a *guide*— someone who says, "Look, I'm heading down Broadway right now, so hop into my car and I'll take you there."

In this chapter we have focused on the nature of God's will. It involves an intimate relationship with Christ more than God's itemized responses to our various questions. We have seen that God's will is mostly a matter of being like Christ and allowing God to be the guide in our thinking process.

On the other hand, there are a lot of other influences besides God that impact our thinking processes. Some of them are benevolent, like our parents and friends. Our culture is also a significant influence, even though we need to "filter" it carefully since it isn't very Christlike. And our thought processes are influenced by our own desires, which at times may be Christlike but at other times are self-centered.

You might be wondering how it is possible to sift through all of the influences and tune in on what God wants us to know. That is an interesting question, and we'll tackle it in the next chapter.

CHAPTER 5

Seven Ways to Figure Out
What God Wants

God does not reveal his will
to curiosity seekers.

—Russ Johnston

Imagine yourself dead for a minute. Not in a "Gee, I wish I was dead" sort of way, but in a "What will they say about me when I'm dead?" kind of way. How will others remember you? What will they write on your tombstone? Will it be something pithy?

> *He died as he lived.*
> —Billy the Kid

> *And away we go.*
> —Jackie Gleason

> *That's all, folks.*
> —Mel Blanc

Or will it be something more poetic?

> *Here lies the body of Frederick Blake*
> *Stepped on the gas pedal*
> *Instead of the brake.*
>
> * * *
>
> *Margaret Daniels:*
> *She always said her feet were killing her*
> *But nobody believed her.*
>
> * * *
>
> *Under the sod and under the trees*
> *Lies the body of Jonathan Pease.*
> *He is not here, there's only the pod,*
> *Pease shelled out and went to God.*

Some may think this little epitaph exercise is morbid. We disagree. Thinking about the end of your life is good for you, because it forces you to think about your life *now*. It's too late to plan for greatness (as defined by God) when you've got one foot in the grave. Rather than waiting until tomorrow, you've got to do something about it today.

Living your life with the end view in mind will bring new meaning to your life. Can you imagine an architect designing a building without first having a vision of the finished product? Would a chef work hard to create a meal unless she knew in advance what it would taste like? Is there a professional athlete out there who doesn't play the game with the end view of winning in mind? Why should your life be any different? Unless you are living your life right and making the right choices now, you won't have the best possible outcome. Neither will you get everything you can get out of life (live to the extreme) *right now!*

God's Eternal Will: Just Accept It

If you don't have the end view of your life in mind right now, don't worry (we'll give you until the end of this chapter). You can rest assured that God does. God sees the big picture of your life—past, present, and future. He wants the best possible outcome for you, and he has already laid it out. All you have to do is respond and choose.

A little later in this chapter, we're going to give you seven principles to help you make good choices when it comes to the details of life. Right now, we'd like to remind you of something we said in Chapter 4: God has an eternal will for you, which will provide a foundation for other life choices.

- *God wants you to accept Jesus as your Savior.* This is the only plan God has for cleaning up your *past*. There's nothing you can to do change it, short of letting God fix it through Jesus Christ. This is the most important choice you can make in your life.

- *God wants you to become more like Jesus.* This is God's plan for your *present*. God doesn't want you to just exist. He wants you to live your life to the fullest every day as you make your choices from his perspective, not yours.

- *God wants you to live with Jesus forever.* A fulfilled life on earth is just the beginning of your eternal life. Jesus is in heaven right now preparing a place for you (see John 14:2). This isn't a fairy tale. It's God's very real plan for your *future*.

This is God's *eternal* will for you. He's got your front and your back covered, and you don't have to do a thing to qualify. All you have to do is accept his eternal will and abide in the results.

If you've made the excellent choice to accept God's eternal will, you probably don't worry too much about the far-off future. It's probably the *present* that gives you fits. This is where the rubber meets the road, so to speak. This is life in the fast lane, and you're behind the wheel. You don't want to drive around aimlessly, and neither do you want to set your life on cruise control. You want to live a life filled with meaning and purpose. You want to make choices that matter—every day.

Seven Steps to Doing God's Will

Pretend your life is a movie for a moment (you can cast anyone you like to play you). God's eternal will takes care of the beginning and end (both very important, by the way). As the Divine Director, God has worked everything out. All he needs is for you to sign off on his plan.

By comparison, God's everyday will deals with the stuff in the middle, otherwise known as the plot of your life. This is the part that really gets interesting, because it involves all the characters, the locations, and the circumstances of your life. As the Divine Director, God has some definite ideas as to what he wants you to do. You could say he has already storyboarded them out (see Ephesians 2:10). But nothing is in cement, because he wants you to make choices. God wants you directly involved in the plot of your life, which he allows you to do through the daily decisions you make.

The possibilities seem endless, and indeed they are. Because even though you are never out of God's sovereign care, he has given you the freedom to discover what it is he wants you to do every day of your life. This is what we mean by doing God's everyday will, and it begins now.

Make no mistake about it. Doing God's will isn't easy. Often it's complicated. Sometimes it's frustrating. But just like anything worth doing, God's will is always rewarding. Furthermore, God will never lead you astray. He may not reveal his everyday will when you think you need it, but he will show you when he knows you need it. Be patient. Wait for God's best. When it comes to timing and God's will, remember:

God is always on time.

Having said that, there are some reliable methods for determining the will of God for you in a particular situation. We have collected seven principles (all of them start with the letter "P"!) from a variety of people who are a lot wiser than we are when it comes to this stuff (OK, so they are a lot wiser than we are when it comes to a lot of stuff). You might want to list these seven principles on a note card and keep them handy so you can refer to them whenever you are faced with a major decision (obviously, this doesn't include your decision to include fries with your next Happy Meal). You could also use these principles to evaluate an opportunity or to solve a problem. As you study them, keep in mind that God wants you to use your mind as you determine to do his will.

Don't act thoughtlessly, but try to understand what the Lord wants you to do.

EPHESIANS 5:17

Principle #1: Precepts

Most of God's everyday will for you is contained in his Word, the Bible. People who are continually frustrated by not knowing God's will usually don't know the Bible. They don't read it regularly and they don't study it systematically. Don't make this mistake. As you live your life as a Christ follower, it's important to live in the light of God's Word. Otherwise you're just dancing in the dark.

Your word is a lamp for my feet and a light for my path.

PSALM 199:105

The Bible contains many *precepts,* which Chuck Swindoll calls "specific, black-and-white truths that take all the guesswork out of the way." Here's an example of a biblical precept:

Let there be no sexual immorality, impurity, or greed among you. Such sins have no place among God's people. Obscene stories, foolish talk, and coarse jokes—these are not for you.

EPHESIANS 5:3

"These specific things are stated to be the will of God," writes Swindoll.

The Bible also contains *principles*. Principles are more general than precepts and serve as general guidelines to assist us through the gray areas. Here's an example:

> *For though your hearts were once full of darkness, now you are full of light from the Lord, and your behavior should show it! For this light within you produces only what is good and right and true.*
>
> EPHESIANS 5:8, 9

Following God's principles requires spiritual maturity and good judgment, which come when you know God's Word.

Principle #2: Prayer

God talks to us most clearly through the Bible, his personal message to us. The way we talk with God is through prayer. King David wrote: "The Lord will answer when I call to him" (Psalm 4:3). "Devote yourselves to prayer," wrote the apostle Paul (Colossians 4:2). And Jesus, who spent more time in prayer than anyone else, said: "Keep on asking, and you will be given what you ask for" (Matthew 7:7).

Are you anxious to know God's will? Do you wonder what you should do in a particular situation? Pray to God about it. Ask him for an answer. But realize this: if you want to know God's will for you, you need to pray according to his will.

> *And we can be confident that he will listen to us whenever we ask him for anything in line with his will.*
>
> 1 JOHN 5:14

This isn't a circular argument. Praying according to God's will means you will never ask God for something you know is contradictory to his nature or his Word. Praying according to God's will also means praying with faith, trusting that God has your best interest in mind at all times.

The earnest prayer of a righteous person has great power and wonderful results.

JAMES 5:16

Principle #3: Prompting

When it comes to knowing and doing God's will, the Holy Spirit is your secret weapon. He's the inside source "who leads into all truth" (John 14:17). Sometimes the words "prompting," "conviction," and "still small voice" are used to describe the Holy Spirit's work in a person's life. Those are fine, but they can be a little subjective. What if the "prompting" you feel late at night is the aftereffect of the double cheese pizza you had for dinner?

"Prompting" makes sense but only in a certain context: to the extent we allow the Spirit to control us (see Ephesians 5:18). When we give our life over to God, whatever we do is done to the glory of God (see 1 Corinthians 10:31). If we faithfully read the Bible and pray, and ask God to do what he wants in and through us, it becomes easier for the Holy Spirit to guide us and for God to speak through our inner promptings.

Principle #4: Present

By *present* we mean *now*. At any given moment you are connected to a variety of people, places, and events, and they are constantly changing. Life is fluid, not stationary.

If you want to know God's will for you today, you need to be aware of what's going on around you. "Look around you!" Jesus told his disciples. "Vast fields are ripening all around us and are ready now for the harvest" (John 4:35). As a Christ follower eager to do God's will, you need to open your eyes today and see God at work. In *The Will of God as a Way of Life*, Gerald Sittser writes:

> The will of God concerns the present more than the future. It deals with our motives as well as our actions. It focuses on the little decisions we make every day even more than the big decisions we make about

the future. The only time we really have to know and do God's will is the *present moment.*[3]

This gets us back to the principle of God's will being a circle rather than a dot. There are so many opportunities and so many needs around you right now, you can just about take your pick. Of course, you need to be wise and thoughtful, especially when it comes to doing God's work. Don't just rush into something because it seems like the right thing to do at the time. As you stay in the Word, pray constantly, and listen to the Holy Spirit (see how these principles build on each other?), the choices you make today will be in line with God's will.

Principle #5: People
Maybe you're in the Word, your prayer life is in tiptop shape, and you feel as though the Holy Spirit is prompting you to do something—but you're still not absolutely sure. Are you lacking faith? Not necessarily. More likely, you need a little more confirmation. That's where the wise counsel of qualified people comes into play. King Solomon, the wisest man who ever lived, didn't rely on his superior judgment and intellect alone. He sought out trusted advisers.

Plans go wrong for lack of advice; many counselors bring success.

PROVERBS 15:22

Though good advice lies deep within a person's heart, the wise will draw it out.

PROVERBS 20:5

As iron sharpens iron, a friend sharpens a friend.

PROVERBS 27:17

God doesn't expect you to make big decisions on your own. He has put people around you—your family, your friends, your pastor, your teachers, and even your boss—to give you advice and help you see things clearly. Ultimately the decision to follow God's will is yours, but remember that God uses others to help you know what his will is.

Principle #6: Peace

It used to be when you bought a car that you had a seven-day "cooling off" period, which was supposed to give you a chance to change your mind after you signed on the dotted line for that spiffy new Daewoo. The automobile manufacturers have stopped that practice (they were getting too many Daewoos back), but you can still incorporate a "cooling off" period into your decision-making process. Especially when you make big decisions that involve things like mortgages, engagement rings, and laser surgery, you need to step back and give God a chance to confirm your decision before you move ahead.

How does God do this? Sometimes he uses your inner organs to give you a strong clue (we're not kidding). If you are about to make a big decision (or you have already made it), and you find your stomach in knots, then you may want to go back through the decision-making principles to see if you missed anything. On the other hand, if your stomach feels fine and you have peace in your heart, then your decision is probably a good one. (Note: Don't get caught in the "Ignorance is bliss" trap. Your peace is valid only if you have followed the other principles in your decision making.)

Principle #7: Pitfalls

Just like anything worth doing well, the will of God carries with it some pitfalls. For example, it's possible to become too subjective in the decision-making process. We put off doing God's will because it just doesn't *feel* right. In *Affirming the Will of God*, Paul Little advised: "We must not feel that every decision we make must have a subjective confirmation."

Another pitfall involves taking Bible verses out of context to confirm what we want God's will to be. Still another pitfall is to assume that being in

God's will makes our lives stress-free. That's just not true. God never promises a life free from stress or trials (in fact, he guarantees just the opposite). What God promises is that he will get us through the difficult times.

So if you are suffering according to God's will, keep on doing what is right, and trust yourself to the God who made you, for he will never fail you.

1 PETER 4:10

The biggest pitfall of all is one we all have to carefully watch. Once you find God's will, be prepared to do it. Refusing to do God's will when you know what it is (and this includes the precepts and principles of Scripture) is in direct disobedience to God, which is nothing less than sin.

Remember, it is sin to know what you ought to do and then not do it.

JAMES 4:17

Go With God, Do With God

God wants nothing more than for you to follow him by following his will. Remember, he is your guide, not your warden. He wants you to follow the principles he has provided, but he won't force you. God isn't waiting for you to step out of his will so he can smack you with a spiritual shovel. He wants to come alongside you as you move forward, making wise choices along the way.

This is what Gerald Sittser calls the "startling conclusion" of God's will. Contrary to what many people think, God hasn't hemmed us in when it comes to his everyday will. As long as we are seeking him with a desire to do his work on earth, as long as our desires are in line with his desires for us, "then *whatever choices we make concerning the future become the will of God for our lives.*" Sittser concludes:

There are many pathways we could follow, many options we *could* pursue. As long as we are seeking God, all of them can be God's will for our lives, although only one—the path we choose—actually becomes his will.

In the next chapter we're going to see how this incredible freedom applies to the very important matter of listening to God's call as you choose a career.

CHAPTER 6

Living to Please

Don't consider how many you can please, but whom.

—Publius Syrus

Every one of us lives to please other people. It's how we gain approval, and all of us need approval. We need our boss, our spouse, or our friends to tell us, "Hey, that was really great," or, "You are da man," or, "You go, girl." When others approve of what we do, we feel encouraged. We're energized.

We're so hungry for approval that we even seek it from complete strangers. Have you ever gone to a fancy restaurant with a menu full of unfamiliar food options? You're reluctant to ask your snooty waiter's advice (you don't want to appear like a country bumpkin), so you close your eyes and point, secretly hoping that he will approve of your choice.

You at the Fancy Restaurant: I'll have the rack of magpie with a hint of pepper spray, followed by a platter of moldy cheese bits from a Parisian garbage dump.

Snooty Waiter: Excellent choice! Your sense of style and taste are magnificent. I salute you!

Boy, doesn't that just make your day? Even if the food you ordered tastes like cardboard, it's worth it just to have the approval of someone who thinks he's better than you.

Does It Really Matter What Someone Else Thinks?

Have you ever let someone down, someone you really care about? It's as if all the air is knocked out of your lungs. You become deflated and discouraged, and start to obsess about what it's going to take to make things right again.

In order to avoid these devastating feelings, some people act as if they don't care about what others think (at least in public). They proudly adopt the "all or nothing" philosophy that says, "You can't please everybody, so you may as well please yourself."

Other, more sensitive individuals go the other route. They go to great lengths never to disappoint, inconvenience, or displease anyone. Even when a complete stranger makes totally unreasonable demands, these "people-pleasers" anxiously bend over backwards to win that person's approval.

Most likely you live somewhere in between these two extremes. You want to please others, but your primary concern is that *you* feel good about what you're doing. You don't want to live only for yourself, but neither do you want to live your life constantly doing what others expect you to do.

If that wasn't enough of a challenge, you have a third factor to consider if you have decided to build your life around the will of God: You want to please God as well. This is where it gets interesting because these three options—pleasing God, pleasing others, or pleasing yourself—sometimes conflict, forcing you to choose. If you don't think this "trilemma" makes your life more complicated than the person who doesn't involve God in the process, consider these three scenarios:

Scenario #1: The Case of the Creepy Boss. Let's say you're in a job with tremendous potential. As the company grows, you will grow, too, both in your career and your net worth. Your boss is a little eccentric, but he's the kind of person who builds big companies quickly by the sheer force of his personality.

Your boss takes you and the management team to Paris to get some funding from a multinational company. He needs the outside investment to keep the company going, so he's been selling the French a little more sizzle than steak. However, your boss doesn't want to let on that his management team still has some development to do before his company is worth what he's asking. So he asks you and the team to fudge a little on the results of your projects. He's not asking you to lie, but he does want to make the company look a little better than it is.

Hey, all the companies looking for capital play this game, and you really like working for this company, but you are more than a little uncomfortable. As the big meeting approaches, you are faced with a choice. Do you go along with your boss this one time, or do you remain true to yourself?

Scenario #2: The Case of the Pressuring Parents. You're going to graduate from college next semester, and your parents are pressuring you to go to law school. You father is a high achiever, and he has always expected a lot from his kids. Your older sister followed the path your parents laid out for her, but you have no interest in law school. In fact, you want to go to seminary so you can become a youth pastor.

You share this with your father, hoping he will understand. Not only does he not understand, but he also threatens to cut off all your support for school, starting now. You pray about it, you search the Scriptures, and you talk to some mature Christians you respect. All the signs and advice point to following your heart and becoming a youth pastor. What do you do?

Scenario #3: The Case of the Neglected Spouse. You graduate at the top of your class with an MBA and marry your college sweetheart. You and two classmates then start a company that takes off like a rocket. Your job is to market the company to investors and advertisers, so you end up traveling more than half the time, and when you're home you work 60-

80 hours a week. Your efforts pay off, and within two years you have exceeded your five-year goals.

Your wife has a baby, which creates a tremendous tension between your family and your job. You want to do both well. Then one day your wife asks you to compare the person you are now to the person she married. She says she loves the person she married. What do you do?

We're not making these stories up. These are people we know, and these were their actual situations. You'll notice in each scenario the main character faced the classic trilemma: pleasing others, themselves and God. For what it's worth, in each case our friend made the decision to please God, but it wasn't easy. We'd like to tell you that everything worked out perfectly, but that's not what happened.

- In order to please God, our friend in Paris stuck to his principles and refused to lie for his boss. Even though others on the team did some fudging, the company did not get the funding, and six months later it was out of business.

- In order to please God and follow her heart, our friend went to seminary and is a youth pastor today. Her parents have basically cut her out of the family.

- In order to please God and his wife, our friend the entrepreneur chose to leave his own company, but he had to leave his equity behind. Today his former company is struggling, and his shares are worth next to nothing.

So what's the lesson for the rest of us? We can think of at least two. The first one has to do with making the right choices:

Making the right choice doesn't always ensure that everything will work out fine.

The second lesson has to do with pleasing God:

Pleasing God doesn't always lead to pleasant situations.

Those two lessons don't exactly make you want to rush out and make choices that are pleasing to God, do they? Truthfully, doing the right thing doesn't seem all that attractive, does it? No wonder so many people—including a lot of Christians—choose to avoid this difficult path. Instead, they make decisions based on what's best for now rather than the future. They concentrate on benefits rather than consequences. Why? We're glad you asked!

Why We Should Please God ... and Why We Don't

By its very definition, *pleasing* someone means to give that person pleasure by doing (or being) what he or she wants us to do (or be). And who better to please than God? He made us in his image, knows us completely, loves us unconditionally, and wants us to live with him eternally. No other being in the universe has so much interest in us. We should want to please God and become what he wants us to be. But we don't.

Every day we are caught on the horns of the great trilemma. Our desire to please people pulls at us, our desire to please ourselves pulls at us, and our desire to please God pulls at us. So why doesn't God win every time? There are two reasons.

We don't please God because we don't think we have to. Yes, it's true that there's nothing we can do to earn God's favor. He saves us by his grace through the person and work of Jesus. It is the gift of God, which we accept by faith (see Ephesians 2:8-9). There's nothing we can do to get God to love us any more, and there's nothing we can do to diminish God's love. He loves us at the fullest capacity, because God is love (see 1 John 4:8).

And yet, the Bible makes it very clear that pleasing God is our responsibility. Our highest priority should be to become what God wants us to be. It's God's will for us to:

Try to find out what is pleasing to the Lord.

EPHESIANS 5:10

Our purpose is to please God, not people. He is the one who examines the motives of our hearts.

1 THESSALONIANS 2:4

Finally, dear brothers and sisters, we urge you in the name of the Lord Jesus to live in a way that pleases God, as we have taught you.

1 THESSALONIANS 4:1

We don't work hard to please God because we don't think he expects us to please him. But he does.

We don't please God because we don't know how. Trying to please God may seem like trying to buy a gift for Bill Gates. What do you give the person who has everything? How do you please God, who demands perfection? Actually, it is impossible to please God, except for one thing:

So, you see, it is impossible to please God without faith.

HEBREWS 11:6

Faith is the key to believing in God in the first place, and it's the key to pleasing God. When we believe by faith that God wants to live through us in a powerful way, he will give us the desire to please him.

For God is working in you, giving you the desire to obey him and the power to do what pleases him.

PHILIPPIANS 2:13

Once we realize that God wants us to please him, we have to understand that we can't please God on our own. He must work in us to give us the desire, and then God must work through us to produce the kind of life that he will be pleased with.

Controlled by the Holy Spirit

If you're getting the impression that God does all the work, you're right. But don't think for a minute that you just sit there and do nothing. Before God can work in you to please him, you have to make a decision. You have to decide if you want the Holy Spirit to control your life or if you want to control your own life.

We'll talk about what happens when you control your life in a minute. First let's look at what happens when the Holy Spirit controls your life.

> *But when the Holy Spirit controls our lives, he will produce this kind of fruit in us: love, joy, peace, patience, kindness, goodness, faithfulness, gentleness, and self-control.*
>
> GALATIANS 5:22-23

Letting the Holy Spirit control you means giving your whole life over to God, so that whatever you do, you are doing it in the will of God and to the glory of God. (We'll talk more about this in the next chapter.) This is when your desires are in line with God's desires, and you begin to think the way God wants you to think. What an extreme way to live!

When your desires match up with God's, you are pleasing him to the extreme. When faced with a decision, you can use your head and follow your heart, confident that God will guide you. The answers or results may not come to you immediately, but you will have a peace that goes beyond understanding.

> *But if the Holy Spirit controls your mind, there is life and peace.*
>
> ROMANS 8:6

Controlled by Your Sinful Nature

God is the one who works in us through the Holy Spirit, enabling us to desire him, please him, and do the things he wants us to do. But we must respond by choosing the Holy Spirit's control. If we don't, then there's only one alternative, and that's to live in the control of our sinful nature (think of it as our spiritual default setting). Even though we are saved and our sins are forgiven, we are still influenced by sinful desires, which are incapable of pleasing God.

> *Those who are still under the control of their sinful nature can never please God.*
>
> ROMANS 8:8

That's because our sinful natures produce all kinds of junk that displeases God in all kinds of ways:

> *When you follow the desires of your sinful nature, your lives will produce these evil results: sexual immorality, impure thoughts, eagerness for lustful pleasure, idolatry, participation in demonic activities, hostility, quarreling, jealousy, outbursts of anger, selfish ambition, divisions, the feeling that everyone is wrong except those in your own little group, envy, drunkenness, wild parties, and other kinds of sin.*
>
> GALATIANS 5:19-21

Does any of this sound familiar? Of course it does! We've all been there, and we'll stay there—even as Christians—unless we make the effort to choose Jesus every day. The apostle Peter addressed this issue in a letter "to all of you who share the same precious faith we have, faith given to us by Jesus Christ, our God and Savior, who makes us right with God" (2 Peter 1:1).

Three Important Steps to Extreme Living

Being right with God is the first and most important step in the process of salvation, but it isn't the only step. God doesn't just save us eternally; he also saves us daily from our sinful desires by giving us the power we need to live a life that's pleasing to him.

> *As we know Jesus better, his divine power gives us everything we need for living a godly life. He has called us to receive his own glory and goodness! And by that same mighty power, he has given us all of his rich and wonderful promises. He has promised that you will escape the decadence all around you caused by evil desires and that you will share in his divine nature.*
>
> 2 PETER 1:3-4

Do you see the part we play in this? We have to *receive* the glory and goodness of Jesus. We have to choose to live in his power and under his control. This is the path to spiritual maturity. This is the way to have a life that pleases God. Here are three steps you can take to stay on the path of spiritual growth. We suggest that you do them every day!

1. *Commit to doing the will of God.* When it comes to doing the will of God, a lot of people play "Let's Make a Deal" with God. They say to God, "Tell me what your will is, and then I'll decide if I want to do it or not." Well, guess what? God doesn't play that game; so don't play that game with God. In his little book *How to Know the Will of God,* Russ Johnston wrote: "God does not reveal his will to curiosity seekers." If you're curious rather than serious about God's everyday will, you'll never know what it is.

   Committing to the will of God involves trusting God. You have to trust that God has your best interests in mind at all times. He knows you better than you know yourself, and he knows what's best for you. God knows your weaknesses, and he knows your strengths. God knows your fears, and he knows your hopes. God will never mislead you or do you harm.

"For I know the plans I have for you," says the Lord. "They are plans for good and not for disaster, to give you a future and a hope."

JEREMIAH 29:11

Trusting God for your future begins with trusting God now step-by-step. And you don't have to wait long for the payoff. Once you have committed to do God's will—regardless of what it is—God will show you what it is step-by-step.

Trust in the Lord with all your heart; do not depend on your own understanding. Seek his will in all you do, and he will direct your paths.

PROVERBS 3:5-6

2. *See things from God's perspective.* You know how important it is to get a bird's-eye view of things. Before you explore New York at ground level, it's important to study a map so you can find your way around. Before you decide to major in quantum physics, you need to read the course descriptions so you can determine if your strengths fit the requirements. The same principle applies to God's everyday will: you need to get a "God's-eye" view before you can do it.

This is going to sound a little contradictory, but hear us out. When you insist on doing God's will from your perspective, then your main concern is *doing.* You get caught up in your own performance. By contrast, when you do God's will from his perspective, you are more concerned about *being.* God wants you to do stuff for him, but he's more interested in the kind of person you are becoming than the specific things you are doing. He knows that when your *being* is right, then your *doing* will be right. And when your *doing* is right, then God gets the credit he deserves, no matter what it is you're doing.

Whatever you eat or drink or whatever you do, you must do all for the glory of God.

1 CORINTHIANS 10:31

3. Let God work in you. The final thing God wants you to know is that you don't have to do his will all by yourself. God has promised to help you.

For God is working in you, giving you the desire to obey him and the power to do what pleases him.

PHILIPPIANS 2:13

What would you do if Bill Gates came to you and said, "I believe in you so much that I'm going to put all of my wealth and power at your disposal to help you succeed"? Would you accept Bill's offer (even if you don't do Windows)? Of course you would!

So here's God (whose wealth and power make Mr. Gates look like a pimple on an elephant's backside), and he's saying, "I believe in you so much that I'm going to put all of my resources at your disposal to help you succeed." Should you accept God's offer? Absolutely!

I pray that from his glorious, unlimited resources he will give you mighty inner strength through his Holy Spirit. And I pray that Christ will be more and more at home in your hearts as you trust in him.

EPHESIANS 3:16-17

When Pleasing Others Pleases God

Earlier in the chapter we posed some scenarios where pleasing others came into conflict with pleasing God. When we're faced with these situations, God asks that we give him priority. But that doesn't mean that we ignore people altogether. God doesn't want us to insulate ourselves in some kind of spiritual isolation chamber, where we only listen to him and never heed the advice or notice the needs of others. In the words of the classic song, we shouldn't be so heavenly minded that we're no earthly good.

God wants us to please him above all else, but he also wants us to please others. In fact, when we please others, we please him, as long as we're doing it with the right motive. Here are some examples from Scripture:

- We need to please others by building them up in the Lord (see Romans 15:2).
- God is pleased when we do good and kind things for others (see Colossians 1:10).
- God is pleased when we obey our parents (see Colossians 3:20).
- We please God when we share what we have with those in need (see Hebrews 13:16).
- Pleasing others can help bring them to salvation (see 1 Corinthians 10:33).

When most people think about pleasing others, they think about what they can get in return, but that's not what God is all about. God wants us to please others by thinking about what we can do for them, not what they can do for us. Our motive should be one of love and self-sacrifice, especially when it comes to loving other Christians.

As people who claim to know and follow Christ personally, our defining characteristic as far as the world is concerned is the love we have for one another. Jesus said: "Your love for one another will prove to the world that you are my disciples" (John 13:35).

So we have come full circle in this whole matter of living to please. We have to resist the urge to please others for selfish reasons. Instead, we must live to please God by asking him daily to give us the desire. When God gives us the desire to please him, he also gives us the desire to please others by loving them sacrificially, just as Christ loved us. This isn't an easy process, but it is incredibly rewarding. And it's the only way for us to be pleased on a personal level. It's the only way to find true meaning and fulfillment.

CHAPTER 7

Your Career:
God's Call or Your Choice?

Find something you like to do so much
that you would gladly do it for nothing.
Then learn to do it so well that people
would be happy to pay you for doing it.

—John C. Maxwell

An important thing happened when you turned to this page. We're bringing it to your attention because it is so subtle that you might have missed it. Assuming that you actually read the first six chapters (which might be a presumptuous assumption on our part), you have finished the first half of the book, in which we focused on "being an extreme person." Now you are embarking on the second half of the book about "doing extreme things." We'll take the theology of God's will out of the ivory tower and bring it down to where you live.

We suspect that a major part of your life revolves around your job, so we'll begin the practical applications of God's will with that subject. After all, if we don't count eight hours a night for sleeping, then about half of your life is spent at work. (It may be less than half if you do some of your sleeping at work so you have more discretionary time in the evening.)

Somewhere along their occupational journey, most Christians end up asking themselves a question like, "I wonder if this is really what God wants me to be doing?" This is a very legitimate and spiritually insightful question. As we discussed in the preceding chapters, God's general will for your life involves becoming more Christlike, so you won't want to be involved with a job—or anything else for that matter—that drives you in the opposite direction.

However, sometimes the question is asked when the job itself violates no spiritual principles, but you just don't like your current circumstances. Or perhaps you have some genuine questions about other issues related to your job:

- Am I working at the right job in my chosen career?
- Forget the job. Am I in the wrong *career?* How do I know if I'm doing what God wants me to be doing?
- Should the salary be a factor in choosing a job, or would that be too materialistic? (We've noticed that questions about being in God's will are more likely to come up after a negative performance review than after receiving a hefty raise.)
- Am I able to put my abilities and gifts to use in this job? What kinds of jobs appeal to me? Should I go by my *desires?* Or are there more spiritual criteria to use in choosing a job?
- Some people say they were "called by God" to a particular position. If I don't think God has "called" me to a particular job, does it mean he is unhappy with where I am?
- And (the granddaddy of all "What is God's will for my job?" questions) would God be more pleased with me if I quit this "secular job" and went into "full-time Christian ministry"?

One or more of these questions may be giving you excess stomach acid. But you can stop carrying that roll of Tums in your pocket. By the end of this chapter, you'll be able to disregard a few of these questions, and you'll know how to answer the others.

You Don't Need to Be a Missionary
to Make Your Job "Spiritual"

You already know that God's general will for you is that your thoughts, actions, and attitudes reflect his holiness. In our attempts to live a Christlike life, we often tend to categorize certain activities as "spiritual" and others as "secular." We think that the "spiritual" activities rank high on the God-pleasing scale, while the "secular" activities leave God shaking his head in disappointment.

Consequently, we figure God always wants us going to a prayer meeting (because that is "spiritual"), whereas playing in a soccer game won't put any stars in our heavenly crown. This same mentality often spills over into our evaluation of careers: a full-time Christian job is more pleasing to God than a secular one. (As a matter of fact, calling it a *ministry* makes it sound even more spiritual.) And many Christians imagine a hierarchy within the realm of Christian ministries. (For example, on the "spiritual career scale," a missionary struggling in a third-world foreign country would rank way ahead of a professional sports team chaplain.)

In God's view, there is no arbitrary distinction between spiritual activities and secular ones. If God lives within you, then you are bringing a spiritual element to whatever you do. Of course, there are some activities that should be avoided because they are totally contrary to God's principles (and you don't need us to give you a list). But for all of the others, whether the activity is "spiritual" or not depends upon you. For example, going to a prayer meeting can be a very *unspiritual* activity if you are using it as an opportunity to catch up (and spread) the most recent gossip tidbits. And playing in a soccer game can be a very *spiritual* activity if you reflect the character of Jesus to your teammates when you are intentionally tripped or the ref makes a bad call against you.

A "Christian Job" Is Any Job That Pleases God

Don't ever think that working in a church is more spiritual than working for a plumbing contractor. Reject the notion that being on the payroll of a ministry is more pleasing to God than receiving your paycheck from Microsoft, Met Life, or Max's Deli.

Unfortunately, secular jobs are often disparaged within the Christian community. Some Christian colleges do a disservice to their students by suggesting that God prefers them to enter "the ministry" instead of "worldly" occupations. Some Christian "professionals" reinforce this sentiment. In *The Fight*, John White criticizes this false distinction:

Is every "secular" occupation either second best or frankly suspect, and would all Christians be better off being in "Christian work"? It will not be long before you discover that certain "full-time" Christian workers, while hesitating modestly to come right out and say so, emit verbal and non-verbal signals which tell us they believe that only "full-time Christian service" is in the center of God's will. Only the "professionals" (those who gain their living by the gospel) are really *in*, the rest of us being second-class citizens. Sometimes we even see ourselves as such.

The apostle Paul didn't see anything wrong with having a "secular" job. While he did receive a little financial support from some of those young, first-century churches, his primary occupation was that of a tentmaker. His teachings reinforce the fact that God does not prefer one job over another.

Those first-century Christians had questions similar to yours. When they established a personal relationship with Jesus Christ, they apparently wondered if they should quit their jobs and do something more "spiritual." Paul told them to keep the jobs that they had before they were saved:

You must accept whatever situation the Lord has put you in, and continue on as you were when God first called you.... Are you a slave? Don't let that worry you—but if you get a chance to be free, take it.... So, dear brothers and sisters, whatever situation you were in when you became a believer, stay there in your new relationship with God.

1 CORINTHIANS 7:17, 21, 24

Should a Christian Work for a Non-Christian?

Paul didn't see anything wrong with having a boss who was not a believer. As employees who are Christians, we are supposed to work diligently in our jobs—whether we are working for a ministry or a secular company—because God is our ultimate boss:

Obey your earthly masters in everything you do. Try to please them all the time, not just when they are watching you. Obey them willingly because of your reverent fear of the Lord. Work hard and cheerfully at whatever you do, as though you were working for the Lord rather than for people. Remember that the Lord will give you an inheritance as your reward, and the Master you are serving is Christ.

COLOSSIANS 3:22-24

Paul also made it clear that a Christian employee has opportunities for witnessing in a secular job environment:

Slaves must obey their masters and do their best to please them. They must not talk back or steal, but they must show themselves to be entirely trustworthy and good. Then they will make the teaching about God our Savior attractive in every way.

TITUS 2:9-10

Don't let the references to slavery confuse you. It was a common practice in the Roman Empire in the first century. Paul is not equating your job at the accounting firm with slavery (although you may make that comparison, especially at tax time). However, the principles are still relevant to you. If God was pleased with the first-century Christian slave who served his master diligently, then God can be equally pleased with your conscientious service in your secular employment. You don't have to quit your job and become a missionary to improve your favor with God.

No Matter Where You Work, You Are in Full-Time Ministry

The entire "God's will for my career" is more confusing than it needs to be due to misnomers embedded in Christian lingo. We refer to Christians who are employed by a church or ministry as being in "full-time" Christian service. By default then, everyone else who works at a "non-Christian" job renders his or her Christian service as a "volunteer" or on a "part-time" basis. This is a distinction that God doesn't acknowledge.

If you are a committed Christian, then you are in "full-time" Christian ministry (see Colossians 3:17). It is a 24/7 ministry, and it is unrelated to whether the logo on your paycheck is a cross, a Christian fish sign, or the Golden Arches.

Because you, as a Christian, are already in full-time ministry, you don't have to view your job at the advertising office as a second-class career in God's eyes. It also means that you can't duck your responsibilities for sharing your faith and relegate that to the pastors who "are paid to do it." Just before he left the earth and ascended into heaven, Jesus told his followers to share the Good News about him "to everyone, everywhere" (Mark 16:15). Because you are in full-time ministry, that is your responsibility, and God has given you the mission field of your office and neighborhood.

Waiting for a Call That Never Comes

Often people refer to their life's work as their "calling." This is a fine biblical term, but it is frequently used out of context. If you hear someone talk about being "called by God" to a particular job, don't feel neglected if you have never received such a call for your occupation. The chances are good that you didn't "miss" the call.

In *Decision Making and the Will of God*, Garry Friesen says that there are only three examples in the New Testament that use the word "call" in the context of being directed to a specific job:

1. **Paul was "called" to be an apostle.** The New Living Translation translates this word in both Romans 1:1 and 1 Corinthians 1:1 as being "chosen" by God to be an apostle.

2. **Paul and Barnabas were "called" to be the first missionaries.** In Acts 13:2, we read that the Holy Spirit spoke during a worship service and said: "Dedicate Barnabas and Saul [Paul] for the special work I have for them."

3. **Paul was "called" to take the gospel message to the Gentiles in Macedonia.** As reported in Acts 16:9-10, Paul had a dream in which a man from Macedonia pleaded with him to come to Macedonia. Paul left immediately for Macedonia because he concluded "that God was calling us to preach the Good News there."

Garry Friesen points out the unusual circumstances that distinguish these three "calls" from the occupational direction that we may receive from God:

- *Each instance was communication through some supernatural revelation by God.* When Paul received his "call," God used an audible voice and a bright light (see Acts 9:1-9; 26:12-18). With Paul and Barnabas, the Holy Spirit either spoke audibly to the group or through one of the prophets in the church (see Acts 13:1-2). And the "call" to Macedonia was communicated through a vivid dream (see Acts 16:9).

- *These "vocational calls" were made only to these certain individuals.* There is no record in the New Testament that the other disciples and followers of Christ received "calls" to establish churches and spread the Christian message. But that's exactly what they did.

- *These "vocational calls" were made only to Paul and Barnabas at these certain times.* While the Holy Spirit specifically spoke to them regarding the first missionary journey, the Bible does not attribute the idea of the second journey to a specific "call" by the Holy Spirit; instead, it appears to have been Paul's idea (Acts 15:36). As it turned out, Paul and Barnabas couldn't agree on hiring an intern by the name of John Mark. The issue wasn't whether John Mark was "called" or not but whether he was capable. When we read the other adventures of both Paul and Barnabas, there is no recorded evidence of external supernatural revelation or direction by God.

- *In each instance, the "call" was unexpected.* For example, there had never been "missionaries" before, so God used this method to start the ball rolling. These were not instances where the occupational call followed a normal pattern or flow in the individual's life. In each case, the "call" represented a huge change of direction from what would otherwise have occurred (such as Paul's becoming a Christian instead of continuing to persecute them).

Friesen points out that the "call of God" in a vocational sense plays a minor role in the New Testament. When it occurs, it is never presented as applying to all believers.

If You Don't Hear a Call—Relax

There are a few instances in the Bible when God called a particular person to a particular task. But those were the exceptions. While God might want you in a specific occupational job, don't wait for a "call" that is accompanied by bright lights and an audible voice.

People who say that they have been called to a particular job will probably admit that there were no fireworks involved. They are probably referring to a subjective sense of guidance from God that seems appropriate and in line with his direction and their desires and abilities. And that's what God's will is all about. Your job isn't any different than other areas of your life, as far as God's will is concerned. As Scripture indicates, you are free to select any job that doesn't violate any precept of Scripture or God's specific will that you become more Christlike.

If you are waiting until you hear a "call," you might miss a lot of opportunities to serve God.

Go With What You Like and What You Can Do Well

With the totality of career options available to you, choosing a career (and a specific job within that career) can be a little intimidating. But God doesn't want you to be frustrated, and he certainly doesn't want you to resort to an Ouija board, a horoscope, or a fortune cookie for guidance. Although you have the freedom to choose any occupation that doesn't interfere with your pursuit of holiness, God has given you a few clues for choosing a career that might suit you.

- *God has given you some natural abilities.* Don't be modest. You've got some. Doesn't it make sense that you'll do better at a job that uses your God-given abilities and talents?

- *God gave you a unique personality.* Stay away from those jobs that would require you to be someone you aren't.

- *You are supernaturally equipped with one or more "spiritual gifts"* (Romans 12:6-8; 1 Corinthians 12:8-10). While the purpose of these gifts is to help the church (see 1 Corinthians 12:7), you should consider your specific spiritual gift as you are making career choices. Does your secular job allow you the opportunity to exercise your gift within the church? Do you have a spiritual gift that is best exercised in vocational ministry?

- *What kind of job do you want to have?* God isn't a crusty killjoy who wants you stuck in a job that you hate. He wants you to be happy, so don't rule out jobs that interest you. Remember, your specific desire for a job might be the result of God planting that desire within your heart (Psalm 37:4).

These factors, when combined, can guide you in selecting a career. For example, maybe you are a math whiz and enjoy crunching numbers, but you are shy and self-conscious. You might be much better suited to working as an actuary for a life insurance company rather than the junior high youth director at your church. (But that doesn't rule out serving at your church in some other capacity. Somebody needs to balance the financial books and count the offering.)

Or maybe you have the spiritual gift of preaching and teaching. You may need a job that gives you enough time during the week to study for the lessons or sermon you'll give at church; or maybe you should accept financial support from the church so you can quit your job and have more time for studying and teaching God's Word.

What If God Really Is Asking Me to Be a Pastor or Career Missionary?

As you walk closer with God, you might have a growing desire to serve him in a way that would require leaving your secular employment. While you might be tempted to make a sudden and drastic change (such as closing your frozen yogurt business and moving to Zimbabwe to work in a missionary orphanage), God's will doesn't usually work that way. He tends to guide people along a progressive path.

Start out with a missions trip with your church to Mexico over spring break. If that encourages you, then take a short-term trip for a month or so over the summer with one of the major missions organizations. Look for ways to do missions work in your spare time. Give God an opportunity to confirm your decisions by your experiences and by the comments of the people you are ministering to and with.

As you consider all of these factors in making job choices, wisdom is what you will need the most. If you want wisdom, all you have to do is ask God for it.

If you need wisdom—if you want to know what God wants you to do—ask him, and he will gladly tell you.

JAMES 1:5

The Bible doesn't say that he will give you omniscience (knowing everything), but he will give you the wisdom to know what career and job best fits you and facilitates your service to him.

What if your family or friends don't agree with your decision to become a lawyer or a research technician or a pastor? Good question. We made a statement earlier that pleasing God doesn't always lead to pleasant situations. Even more, pleasing God may involve suffering and setbacks. That's what the next chapter is all about.

CHAPTER 8

Who Do You Blame
When Things Go Bad?

From time to time a great event, ardently desired,
does not take place because some future time
will fulfill it in greater perfection.

—Jacob Burckhardt

This book is all about choices. On the other hand, sometimes our choices lead to results that we did not anticipate. Sometimes they are better than what we expected. Sometimes they are worse. Lots worse.

In this chapter, we'll be looking at choices from a completely different point of view. Until now, we have used a *prospective* perspective. We have discussed how you can analyze your choices *before* you make them. Now we will change gears and take a glance into the rearview mirror. With a *retrospective* perspective, we will evaluate choices already made by examining the results and circumstances they produced.

This is not an uncommon method for evaluating past choices for future reference. Many people call it second-guessing. Others call it hindsight. It happens all of the time, and it is a very customary occurrence in our culture:

- In personnel management, this process is called a "performance review." It evaluates the decisions that were made by the employee.

- Sometimes the approach is even described with terminology related to a particular field of endeavor. For example, when sports fans rehash a football coach's decisions, they call it "being a Monday morning quarterback."

- In some professions, there is an official procedure for the after-the-fact evaluation of choices that produced disastrous results. For surgeons it is called "an autopsy" (unless the evaluation is being conducted by lawyers, in which case it is called "a medical malpractice lawsuit").

We suspect that you are well acquainted with the process of second-guessing choices. You probably do it to yourself all of the time. Well, maybe not *all* of the time. According to our highly unscientific, nonquantitative research methodology (which consists of sitting in Starbucks and listening to the conversations at the tables around us), the hindsight evaluation process is selectively used for certain types of choices. If you are like most people:

- *You never second-guess yourself if the immediate circumstances turn out good.* If everything goes well after you made your choice, you automatically assume it was a good one. You don't take the time to analyze the decision any further. You don't bother to reassess the choice in the context of long-range results that are yet to be realized. You just go on with life.

- *You might second-guess decisions that were recently made, but you don't apply the reassessment process to choices made long ago.* Suppose you logged on to your e-trading brokerage account in January and purchased a NASDAQ stock at $24 per share. When the stock hit $49 per share in March, you felt like a Wall Street wizard. But now it is

September and the stock is at $6 per share. You are feeling like a financial fool for making a bad decision. According to your short-term evaluation, you made a lousy choice when you didn't sell in March. In actuality, it might have been the initial purchase decision that was faulty. But since the immediate consequences after the initial purchase were good, you kept playing the market on the assumption that you were a stock-picking savant when in reality you would have been better off keeping your money in your sock drawer.

- *Even if your choice was an obviously poor one, you don't second-guess yourself if the unpleasant circumstances are inconsequential or brief.* Imagine that you are suffering through a sleepless night because you are bloated and disturbed by gastrointestinal disruptions. You know this is a direct result of a few poor choices that you made earlier in the day. You should have declined that fifth, sixth, and seventh chili cheese dog at the Super Bowl party. But you don't torture yourself about making the wrong decisions. You will merely endure this relatively brief and insignificant discomfort by taking a "sick day" on Monday and swigging down a bottle of Pepto-Bismol.

Those are the types of situations when you decline to use hindsight. But what are the scenarios when you will use a retrospective analysis of your decisions? Well, as it turns out, there is only one type of situation when it occurs:

> ## Most people second-guess their choices only when present circumstances have turned out really bad.

If you are in a dreadful, awkward, or difficult situation following your decision, then you automatically assume that you made "the wrong choice." You embark on an agonizing journey of self-psychoanalysis that usually ends with your berating yourself for stupidity, lack of intuition, and poor judgment. You become so introspective and self-critical that you distrust every other choice that you have made in the last decade. Your life becomes a maelstrom of self-doubt and uncertainty that makes you dissatisfied with every area of your life. (OK, maybe we are exaggerating a bit, but we probably aren't too far off.)

Perhaps you are smack-dab in the middle of difficult circumstances. Maybe you are extremely unhappy with the way things in your life have turned out. You thought that you were making good decisions at the time, but your present situation causes you to believe that you must have made some colossally wrong choices in the past. You are wondering what went wrong in the decision-making process. But hold on a minute. Maybe the problem wasn't with your decisions at all. Maybe you made good choices in the first place but lack a proper perspective on the consequences.

As we said, choices lead to results. But your present circumstances may not be the final results of the choices you have made.

Maybe It's Not Bad. Maybe It's Just Different.

If you say that you are going through a tough situation, we won't argue with you. But we won't be quick to agree with you either. With all due respect, we'd like to suggest that perhaps your situation isn't as bad as you think it is.

Sometimes people are unhappy with their circumstances simply because their current situation isn't what they expected. Everything could be going great, but if it is not what they had anticipated, then they are dissatisfied. When analyzed objectively, their circumstances aren't bad, just different. The unhappiness with the current situation is simply due to a difference between reality and expectations.

Since we don't know the specifics of your situation, we'll get hypothetical with you for a moment to explain the point we are trying to make:

- **Your Reality:** You've got a great job that pays the going rate of $48,000 a year with a long list of perks and benefits. There's lots of opportunity for upward mobility, and your supervisors are pleased with your work.

   Your Expectations: You had always planned on making $60,000 per year at this stage of your career. Because you aren't getting what you had expected (your expectation was unrealistic in the first place), you feel underpaid and unappreciated. You figure that you blew it when you accepted the job offer for your current job.

- **Your Reality:** After graduation from college, you moved out-of-state. You have settled into your new surroundings. You have established some nice friendships at work, and you are active in the career group at your new church. Your job keeps you pretty busy, but you spend one or two evenings a week with friends. You are too tired for much else.

   Your Expectations: When you were in college, you expected that your social life would get better after graduation (just as many friends, but without the nuisance of homework). Now you have *fewer* friends around (because you don't live in a dorm). And you have *less* free time (because it turns out that work is more time-consuming than studying). You are feeling like a social outcast, so you are second-guessing your decision to move away from the college town.

- **Your Reality:** You are twenty-eight years old. You are on the fast track in your career. You just put a down payment on a house. You have a circle of close friends who are very supportive, and you are well liked by a wide network of coworkers and acquaintances. You are involved in several ministries in the community and in your church that bring real meaning to your life. You have had several romantic relationships along the way, but nothing has really clicked yet in that department.

   Your Expectations: You always thought you would be married by now. You can't stand the thought that it might never happen for you. Many of your friends aren't married yet either, but you obsess about the ones who *are* married (or at least engaged). This is *not* what you had in mind at all, and you feel like a big loser.

Maybe we didn't even come close to describing your situation, but you can figure out the "reality vs. expectation" contrast that fits your personal circumstances.

Life usually turns out differently from what you expected. That doesn't mean that the result is bad. Oftentimes the result is better than what you anticipated. But you will never appreciate what you have if you are always disappointed that you didn't get what you had envisioned. So, in the process of analyzing your past choices, make sure that you fairly evaluate your current circumstance. It may not be as bad as it seems.

**If you don't objectively evaluate
your circumstances,
you are likely to
fall apart at the seems.**

Do You Worry What Others Think About You?

You aren't the only one who had expectations for your life. A lot of other people had expectations for you as well. Maybe the opinions of these other people have put a lot of pressure on you:

- You have been working hard to live up to the high expectations of your parents and to make them proud of you.
- You vowed to yourself that you would transcend the low expectations of your in-laws and make them regret their predictions of "prison or poverty by age 35."
- That designation of "most likely to succeed" in your high-school yearbook feels like a noose around your neck. The next reunion is approaching, and the noose is getting tighter.

- You left your hometown to achieve success in the big city. As it turns out, you don't like the big city and you are qualified for a great job back home. If you had stayed in town and worked up to the job, you'd be a success. But you didn't. And when you left, you made a big deal about "making it on your own." If you move back home, everyone will assume that you didn't have what it takes to make it in the outside world.

Maybe you are unhappy with your current circumstances because you are afraid of what other people will think. Don't let that happen. Evaluate your circumstances based on what *you* want out of life. If you are dissatisfied with your current situation, then you can do something about it. But don't go rearranging your life based on the opinion of others.

Input from friends and family is an important part of the decision-making process. But there are three important reasons why your choices shouldn't be dictated—or even strongly influenced—by the opinions of other people outside your immediate support group:

1. *Other people aren't thinking about you as much as you imagine.* Sure, you occupy the thoughts of a few family members and a few close friends. But the rest of the population of the world goes through life without regard to what you do. If someone bothers to think about you at all—even if it is in a critical way—he or she is soon distracted by something more important (like the cost of a utility bill, the score of yesterday's game, or today's Dilbert cartoon).

2. *You will never know what they are actually thinking.* You imagine that they will analyze your life choices and come to some conclusion about your intellect, integrity, or initiative. But they aren't thinking that deeply about you. Their analysis is much more shallow than that. They are only checking up on you to make sure that your clothes match and that you aren't spreading gossip about them.

3. *Their opinion doesn't really matter.* Before you let yourself get too unhappy with your present situation, make sure that your evaluation is

based upon what you want and is not influenced by your fear of what others may think about you.

Everyone has a right to his or her own opinion, but it is generally of no use to anyone else.

God May Not Be Finished Yet

We know that there are lousy circumstances in life. Not all situations can be made acceptable by simply adjusting your expectations or disregarding the opinions of others. When such events occur in your life, the pain cannot be minimized by a change of perspective. The sorrow or grief does not quickly subside with the passage of time.

As we were writing this section of this chapter, we heard a young mother tell a part of the story of her life. It was a story of difficult health challenges that obliterated any control she had over the events of her life. We appreciated her honesty when she said that her initial reaction was to question whether God was really in charge. As her situation continued to get worse with absolutely no promise of relief, she began to have doubts about God:

- Maybe he is not in control after all; or
- Maybe he isn't paying attention to what is happening; or
- Maybe he really doesn't care.

She knew and believed the Bible, so she was able to intellectually dismiss these thoughts. But she also knew that God was sovereign and that all circumstances are within his ultimate control. The doctrine of God's sovereignty, however, didn't comfort her. In fact, it made her mad. She admitted to being "angry with God." He was able to change her circumstances and give her relief, but he was refusing to do so.

As we listened intently, we expected her to reveal a spirit of bitterness toward God. But she said her anger with him turned to thankfulness when she realized that God was actively and lovingly working in her life. He wasn't changing her circumstances, but he was changing *her*. She tearfully acknowledged that God was correcting certain attitudes and emotions in her life that were desperately in need of adjustment. God was changing her on the inside through the use of circumstances on the outside. She proclaimed that she sensed God's love and presence in the midst of her tough situation from the moment she realized that he was bringing a good result out of tragic circumstances.

This woman's story was a real-life sermon on the text of Romans 8:28:

And we know that God causes everything to work together for the good of those who love God and are called according to his purpose for them.

This verse may be of great comfort to you, but only if you absorb the full import of what it says. It does not say that only good things will happen to us; and it does not say that we will be exempt from anything bad. In fact, it implies that bad things will happen. God may allow the full complement of problems in our lives. Don't expect to be spared from financial failings, health problems, broken relationships, setbacks in your career, family heartaches, and other such tragedies. But Romans 8:28 clearly reaffirms the principle of God's sovereignty and declares that he will use those difficult circumstances to achieve a good result in our lives.

> ## The truth of Romans 8:28 will be a comfort only when you can look past your present circumstances to the future results.

Bruce & Stan's "Four-Part Evaluation Square"

If you are tempted to second-guess your choices based on your present circumstances, then we suggest that you use an evaluation process that incorporates the principle of Romans 8:28. In other words, don't base your evaluation solely on your present situation. Remember that God may be using an unpleasant, temporary situation to achieve a beneficial long-term result.

We have developed a matrix to illustrate the importance of evaluating your decisions with a Romans 8:28 perspective.

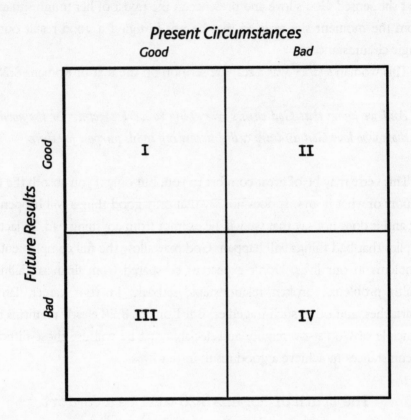

Here's how it works:

- If you are in Quadrant I, both the short-term and long-term effects of your decision are beneficial. You made a good choice.

- You don't want to be in Quadrant IV. Nothing good came from your decision. You had problems right from the start, and things never got better. Bad choice.

- Quadrants II and III are tricky. At first, you might think that a Quadrant II decision was lousy because the immediate circumstances were bad; but it turns out to be a good decision because the long-term effects are beneficial. Conversely, a Quadrant III decision looks good at first, but later seems to be a poor choice because the future results are negative.

The apostle Paul didn't bother to include a matrix diagram on the parchment that he used to write to the Romans. We aren't suggesting that it is biblical (although it is probably a better analytical technique than a coin toss). But you will notice that our matrix requires you to consider the long-term perspective of the choices that you have made. That is the key to Romans 8:28. What appears to be unpleasant for the moment may be the beginning of a process that will have great results.

Don't be quick to escape
what God wants to accomplish in your life.

You need to give God time to work out the details in your life, and that's not going to happen overnight. It probably won't happen as soon as you want. But it will happen. Like a potter who works on a lump of clay with the end view in mind, God is using everything in your life—the good as well as the bad—to create something beautiful and significant.

In the next chapter we're going to expand on this a little more. We want to assure you that the most important changes and improvements in your life are likely to be small and incremental rather than big and monumental. This doesn't mean you sit idly by while God shapes your life. The choices you make—in your relationships, your money, your job, your character, and your relationship with God—are a big part of the process.

CHAPTER 9

Making Choices
That Matter Every Day

Eighty percent of success is showing up.

—Woody Allen

John Lennon once said, "Life happens when you're making other plans." Can you identify with that? We sure can. Whether you're talking about everyday routine activities or long-range plans, things don't always turn out the way you planned them.

You know how it goes. From the minute you wake up in the morning to the moment your head hits the pillow at the end of the day, you are faced with all kinds of surprises, twists and turns, none of which were written down on your daily "To Do" list. (For the record, Bruce has an up-to-date method of keeping track of his appointments and tasks. He uses a Handspring Visor, which he delights in showing off in front of Stan, who keeps his schedule on little pieces of paper wadded up in his pockets.)

And that's just the everyday stuff. When it comes to the big stuff, life rarely turns out the way you think it will. While you're making long-range plans to accomplish future goals, you end up spending most of your time fulfilling past obligations. Just when you think you're ready to follow tomorrow's dreams, you find yourself recovering from yesterday's nightmare. But somehow you get through it, because you realize something Frank Sinatra sang about years ago: "That's life."

Extreme Living Means More Than Just Staying Afloat

The more you experience life, the more you realize that living life is like floating on water in a boat, only you don't get to choose the kind of water you're on. You dream about setting your own course and moving along at your own speed on a nice quiet lake, but the reality is that most of the time your boat is traveling down a river with all kinds of currents and rocks and rapids. As much as you'd like to navigate in any direction, depending on your mood, about all you can do is steer.

We happen to like rivers more than lakes, because with lakes, the scenery never changes (besides, lakes collect mosquitoes), while rivers offer something new around every bend. Steering doesn't matter much on a lake (because no matter which way you steer you eventually reach the shore), but in a river steering is important. Steering is what you use to find the best spots and avoid the worst ones.

We want to concentrate on your steering skills in this chapter; knowing how to steer your boat down the river is like knowing how to make the right choices as your life moves along. If you're in the river, it's going to carry you. If you're alive, life is going to happen. But you're not helpless. There are plenty of things you can do to live your life to the extreme.

The Magic of the Mundane

We have given you lots of advice in this book. Some of it has been pretty profound, such as understanding how God runs the universe and how you fit in (you've got to admit it, that's very profound). We talked about what it takes to please God (and displease him). Finally, in the last chapter we dealt with life's difficulties and how God can use them to build character in your life. That's all profound stuff, and it can be a lot to absorb in just one book. That's why we want to take a break from the profound and talk about the mundane, the everyday stuff, the little things you hardly notice. But don't think the mundane is any less important than the profound. In fact, in many ways it's more important.

God's will is done in the little things of life, daily and locally.

—Larry Sittser

Remember the story of the tortoise and the hare? The moral of the story is simple but true: sure and steady beats fast and jerky every time. Not in the short run, mind you, but in the long run. If life were nothing more than a 100-meter dash, then the rabbit would win every time. But life isn't like that. Life is more of a marathon than a sprint. One step follows another, and every step counts.

The magic of the mundane is this:

**Little things done well every day
add up to much more
than big things done well
every once in a while.**

It's natural to equate extreme living with doing the extraordinary, the spectacular, and the outrageous. We've all seen too many action movies where the hero saves the world and gets the girl in less than two hours. But that's not real life. It's a myth. While others are looking for shortcuts, big payoffs, and quick bucks (why do you think the lottery is so popular?), you need to concentrate on the ordinary, the steady, and the commonplace. That's how big things get done, little by little, and more importantly, that's where God is.

God Is in the Small Stuff

A few years ago we wrote a little book called *God Is in the Small Stuff.* At the risk of shameless self-promotion, we want to share a couple of principles from the book that relate to this chapter on making choices that matter every day. We know these principles are true because they're from God's Word (in other words, we didn't make them up). And we know these principles work because thousands of people have told us how rewarding and comforting it is to know that God is at work in the details of life.

It's easy to see God in the big things of life, from joyous celebrations (such as the birth of a child) to major tragedies (such as losing a loved one). Whether we are at the heights of emotion or the depths of despair, when we turn to God we find him willing to share our joy and give us strength in our sorrow. Either way, we feel close to God.

Now, God shines in the big stuff. But where he really *works* is in the small stuff. We appreciate God in the profound events, but we get to know him in the mundane moments. "What makes God so clear to us," wrote Oswald Chambers, "is not so much his big blessings, but the tiny things, because they show his amazing intimacy with us—that he knows every detail of each of our individual lives."

This is the first principle of *God Is in the Small Stuff:*

The best way to know God is in the everyday details.

The second principle relates directly to the first, and it has to do with the so-called circumstances of life. We say "so-called" because most of us think circumstances just "happen." Even as Christians we get used to using words like "lucky" or "fortunate" to describe little things that happen to us every day (or we call ourselves "unlucky" or say something was "unfortunate" if things go badly).

Truthfully, the circumstances themselves really aren't the issue. Even though God fills the universe with his presence, he doesn't cause a traffic jam just to frustrate you or a beautiful day just to please you. Yes, God is in control of every detail and every circumstance, but he's much more inter-ested in how you respond to the traffic jam or the beautiful day than he is in the jam and the day themselves.

Run the Race to Win

The apostle Paul illustrated these principles in a letter to the Christians in Corinth. The Corinthians of the first century were a lot like those of us in the twenty-first century. They lived in a culture enamored with the spectac-ular and the sensational. Immorality and idolatry were rampant as people looked for the quick road to pleasure rather than the long road to purity. We suggest you read the entire letter sometime (there's all kinds of good stuff about relationships and marriage in there), but we want to focus on the way Paul compared living the Christian life to an athlete engaged in competition.

> *Remember that in a race everyone runs, but only one person gets the prize. You also must run in such a way that you will win. All athletes practice strict self-control. They do it to win a prize that will fade away, but we do it for an eternal prize. So I run straight to the goal with purpose in every step. I am not like a boxer who misses his punches. I discipline my body like an ath-lete, training it to do what it should.*
>
> 1 CORINTHIANS 9:24-27

Notice the words "self-control," "purpose," "discipline," and "training." These are not words you normally associate with extraordinary activity. You are more likely to think of ordinary achievement. Yet when it comes to win-ning the eternal prize, achievement will beat out activity every time.

Never confuse activity with achievement.

No Shortcuts to Success

The way you respond to your circumstances—the way you see God in the small stuff—relates directly to the way you do ordinary things. Do you strive for excellence in everything you do, or do people sometimes use the word "slacker" (behind your back, of course) to describe your habits? Are you so preoccupied with making things happen or getting your "big break" that you miss the little steps along the way?

Let's look at several basic areas of life where it's tempting to take shortcuts. In each case you will see that attention to detail is not only better than inconsistent behavior in the long run, but it is also essential to long-term success.

Relationships

This is where the most basic of all human activities take place. From the day you are born you are in relationships, first with your mother, then with the rest of your family, and then with other people who nurture you and help you develop from a slobbering baby into a functional adult. At some point in your life (before you become an adult, we hope), you realize that building relationships takes time and effort.

If you want to get along with your teachers at school, for example, you learn that staying awake in class and doing your homework every day are much more effective than showing up at class just long enough to ace your final exam. You discover that lasting friendships are built one day at a time over many months and years rather than through occasional contact.

It's how you do in the routine and the mundane that determines the quality of your relationships, not how great you are in the big moments. This is especially true if and when you enter the most intimate human relationship of all: marriage. If your idea of quality relationships is to come in and out of people's lives when it's convenient and fun for you, then marriage is going to be a constant struggle.

Loving another person at the highest level means you are there for that person, seven days a week, twenty-four hours a day. It doesn't mean you are *with* your husband or your wife every minute, but it does mean you are devoted to him or her and available no matter where you are or what you're doing.

Work

Next to your relationships with people, the work you do requires the most time and attention. And we're not just talking about your occupation or your career. Long before you know what it takes to get a paycheck, you are working. You clean your room, make your bed, mow the lawn, put dishes in the dishwasher, walk the dog, baby-sit your little brother, and do your homework. There's nothing exciting about these things, but listen to this:

If you don't learn to do these small things daily and relatively well, you're going to have trouble holding a job when you really need it.

When you get that job, whether it involves flipping burgers or filing papers, your daily attention to detail and routine will be more important than your occasional bursts of brilliance.

Both of us work in professions that require amazing attention to detail. Bruce is a lawyer, which may sound glamorous but is in fact pretty mundane. Forget what you see in *The Practice* or read in John Grisham novels. A lawyer spends relatively little time in the courtroom. A successful law practice is comprised of thousands of little (read: boring) things that have to be done over and over again.

The same goes for Stan's world of retailing. A lot of people dream about owning their own store where they can sell cool stuff and set their own hours. The reality is that retail, like most business ventures, is painfully detailed. It can be rewarding, but not without paying close attention to thousands of products and hundreds of customers every day. Not to mention you have to be there every day to open the store.

Do you dream about having a wonderful and fulfilling career? The best way to get there is to master the routine of whatever you're doing right now.

Develop the art of accountability. Be the person your boss, your coworkers, your clients, and your customers can count on to deliver quality work and excellent service 100 percent of the time.

Money

It usually starts with an allowance or the classic lemonade stand. Somewhere in your young life you learn that people will give you money in exchange for a service you perform or a product you produce. And with that money you can buy fun and necessary stuff, like action figures, video games, CDs, and soda.

Your attitude toward money is shaped from a young age and is heavily influenced by the people around you and the work you do for them. Unfortunately, some kids develop a "get something for nothing" mentality early in life. They figure their parents owe them an allowance, whether or not they lift a finger around the house. (Note to future parents: Kids develop this attitude because parents allow it. Always insist that your kids work for their allowance.)

Somewhere along the way you realize that money doesn't grow on trees. You have to show up for work to get paid, and when you're at work you have to actually get things done. Otherwise the person who signs paychecks will stop giving you one. It doesn't matter where you work or at what level. Your ability to earn money is directly related to your attention to detail and routine. You've got to be there for your boss and your customers. The stuff you do for people must benefit them in some way. The products you make or sell have to actually work.

During the dotcom frenzy, most people entered into that cyber business as if they were buying lottery tickets. Rather than building companies that provided long-term benefits for their customers and long-term value for their investors, these Silicon Valley hotshots figured they could build a fancy Web site, create a cute sock puppet, run a television ad during the Super Bowl and—ka-*ching!*—become millionaires.

Of course, a few people did get rich, but they were the *first* few (like the first few people in a pyramid scheme). Many e-businesses fizzled in a big way because the attitude toward money was wrong. People forgot a fundamental principle: If you are going to build a successful lemonade stand, you have to make good lemonade, and you have to be there when your customers are thirsty.

Character

You don't build character or develop a reputation for excellence by *telling* people how trustworthy or honest or reliable you are. You must *show* them, and that takes time. There are no shortcuts to character, because character is based on your track record. A quality reputation is built one step at a time.

You could compare building character to climbing a ladder. You don't climb a ladder unless you are prepared to concentrate on what you're doing. You take it one step at a time, hold on with both hands, and make sure you've got a good grip. If you've ever slipped while climbing a ladder (especially one of those aluminum ones), you know what happens: you end up back at the bottom (sometimes on your bottom). The only thing you can do is start climbing again, this time doing everything you can to keep from slipping.

That's how you build character. If you want to get from where you are to a higher level of trust and integrity, you don't leap, you don't run, and you don't ask someone else to do your climbing for you. Little by little, step-by-step, you become faithful in the small things done daily. You become the person others can count on to be truthful. You don't live one kind of life in private and another kind in public. You demonstrate that you are the kind of person who does what's right, whether or not someone's watching. And when you slip and let others down, you realize that it's going to take time to build your reputation once again. You may not have to start at the bottom, but you do have to recover, and that starts by being honest with the people you have offended.

God

People sometimes talk about "fearing" God, and there's some truth to that (hey, it's in the Bible—see Proverbs 15:33). However, don't fear him as you would fear someone who wants to harm you. When God says his plans for you are "for good and not for disaster, to give you a future and a hope," he means it (Jeremiah 29:11).

No. Fearing God, according to Chuck Swindoll, means that we take him seriously and do what he says. Most of God's will for us is in his Word, and mostly it has to do with small things done daily: reading the Bible, praying, loving others, and loving God. We don't have to be flashy for God. We don't have to be outrageous. He's not impressed.

The prophet Micah talked about this very thing when he wrote:

> *What can we bring to the Lord to make up for what we've done? Should we bow before God with offerings of yearling calves? Should we offer him thousands of rams and tens of thousands of rivers of olive oil? Would that please the Lord?... No, O people, the Lord has already told you what is good, and this is what he requires: to do what is right, to love mercy, and to walk humbly with your God.*

MICAH 6:6-8

Do you see the beauty in that? God isn't looking for your occasional big sacrifice. He wants your everyday mundane obedience. Don't worry about showing off for God. Just show up. Do what's right, love other people and show them mercy, walk with God in humility, do small things every day. This is what God asks of you. This is what pleases him.

Peace Like a River

We opened this chapter with a little analogy of life flowing like a river, and how important it is to steer as your boat moves along. Now that we're at the end of the chapter, we hope you know what it takes to steer effectively. It isn't dramatically turning your boat from one direction to another. Smooth steering is much more subtle. It's a constant process of making small corrections so you stay on track and avoid the places that could cause your boat to crash.

The other part of steering your life is realizing that God is in the boat with you. He's the captain of your boat, but he's letting you steer. God has plenty of advice, and he gives it to you freely through his Word, other people and the circumstances of your life. But it's up to you to listen and learn. Read what God says:

The LORD, your Redeemer, the Holy One of Israel, says: I am the LORD your God, who teaches you what is good and leads you along the paths you should follow. Oh, that you had listened to my commands! Then you would have had peace flowing like a gentle river and righteousness rolling like waves.

ISAIAH 48:17-18

CHAPTER 10

The Power of
Positive Prayer

Too many people pray like little boys
who knock at doors, then run away.

—Anonymous

The role of prayer usually crops up in any discussion about making choices and determining God's will. Few people would be so bold as to say that prayer is worthless (they might think it, but they would never say so out loud). However, in the context of God's sovereignty, prayer might seem futile. If God already knows what he is going to do, can prayer really accomplish anything?

What's the Point of Prayer?

If you have ever implored God to intervene in a particular situation in your life, you might have wondered about the dichotomy between providence and prayer. Perhaps you asked yourself questions like these:

- Since God knows everything, including what I want, why should I waste his time (and mine) telling him what he already knows?
- And since God already knows how my life is going to turn out, why should I pray if it's not going to change anything?
- If my prayers have an effect on what happens, then how could God's plan be fixed in the first place? Oh, great! Now the pressure is on me to pray hard enough to convince God to do what I want.
- What kind of prayer makes the biggest impression on God? Is once-a-day praying enough, or do I have to get fanatic about it? Do I get weekends off? Would it help if I prayed with a Shakespearean accent?

In his *Christian Theology* treatise, seminary professor Millard J. Erickson has written about the dilemma that arises when Christians consider the nature of God's providence and the role of prayer. In this treatise he points out that there are two inescapable truths:

- God has a definite plan that is not subject to revision. The Bible says so (see Ephesians 1:11).
- The Bible tells us that we are to pray for one another, and that prayer can make a difference (see James 5:16).

But how do these two facts relate to each other? The purpose of this chapter is to answer this very important question. But before we do, we have two other questions—much more basic—that should be answered first:

Do we really know what prayer is?
and
Are we doing it right?

All About Prayer

There are as many approaches to prayer as there are people praying. Some people pray at the drop of a hat—to find a parking place, for instance, or when their favorite team is poised to win the Super Bowl. Others pray mainly when they are in a real jam—something involving hospitals, police, or IRS agents.

Public prayers are especially revealing. Some are fluent in "Churchese," with thunderous, rolling tones that seem to flow from the pulpit (or the pews) to the very gates of heaven. And don't forget the ones who punctuate their prayers with God's name the way most people would use a comma: "Thank you, Jesus, for your love, God, and for sending your Son, Father, into the world to die for us, God ..." (Do they think God isn't listening, or what?)

How you pray says a lot about your relationship with God—and your spiritual maturity. In a way, that's to be expected: the deeper you go in the spiritual life, the more like Jesus you become. However, there's a big difference between how long you've been a Christian and how deep that relationship goes. Here are some prayer approaches that could reveal a heart that needs to "go deeper."

1. *Prayer is like a computer.* These people think of prayer the same way you might use your laptop:

   - They use it on a regular basis;
   - They don't really understand how it works;
   - They complain that it is not working right when they don't get the results that they want (even though the real problem may have been operator error);
   - It makes life a little easier in most circumstances;
   - They believe that they could get along just as well without it by doing the work themselves (although they won't admit it).

2. *Prayer is like room service in a luxury hotel.* To these people, God is some sort of heavenly bellhop who will bring them whatever they want. Just call him up, tell him what we want, and expect him to deliver—pronto! (And prayer is even better than hotel room service because you don't have to tip.)

3. *Prayer is like a visit to your favorite shrink.* These people see prayer a little less materialistically, but their approach is still self-centered. They consider prayer to be therapeutic, a way to purge stress and anxiety from their thoughts and achieve emotional catharsis. Their words just keep pouring out, without much thought behind them, until they feel better.

4. *Prayer is a means of self-motivation.* These people think of prayer as a way to create a positive mental attitude. Once they are psyched up, then they go on their own way without any further dependence upon God. They use God the way a professional athlete uses a sports psychologist: After spending a few moments with him before the game to focus their thoughts, they leave him in the locker room and go play the game.

There is a direct connection between prayer and God's will, but it has nothing to do with our getting what we demand or focusing on our thoughts. Just the opposite. Prayer is all about learning what God wants and absorbing his thoughts. If when we pray we make God the focal point of our lives, we change from being self-centered to being God-centered.

Giving God the ACTS

It is not easy to resist the temptation to make your prayers all about you. Some people use the acrostic ACTS to keep their prayers from being a "gimme" list.

"A" is for adoration: Because of who he is, God is worthy of our worship and praise. The Psalms are a good example of this. David praised God, and his expressions of adoration actually drew him closer to God. Here is how theologian R.C. Sproul describes this aspect of prayer:

> In adoration the focus of our attention is not upon ourselves or upon our own needs. Here the focus is on the glory and majesty of God. We are basking in His glory and delighting in His presence when we are engaged in authentic adoration.

"C" is for confession: God can always hear you when you pray, but if you are rebelliously refusing to admit the wrongs that you have committed, then God is not inclined to listen to your prayers. God loves you, but he hates sin.

You can't defiantly hold on to sin and expect to enjoy an intimate relationship with God. A tolerant attitude toward sin is like static on a cell phone that completely disrupts the conversation. It cuts you off from hearing what God wants to say to you. Since the prophet Isaiah couldn't use a cell phone analogy, he explained it this way:

> *Listen! The Lord is not too weak to save you, and he is not becoming deaf. He can hear you when you call. But there is a problem—your sins have cut you off from God. Because of your sin, he has turned away and will not listen anymore.*
>
> ISAIAH 59:1-2

When you confess your sins to God, you won't be shocking him (he knows all about it, anyway). However, by confessing your faults to him, you remove the stench of hypocrisy that puts a barrier between you and him. So confession is for *your* benefit, not his. It emphasizes his perfect holiness and your unworthiness. That's what makes his love so amazing—that he loves you even though you don't deserve it.

If I had not confessed the sin in my heart, my Lord would not have listened. But God did listen! He paid attention to my prayer. Praise God, who did not ignore my prayer and did not withdraw his unfailing love from me.

PSALM 66:18-20

"T" is for thanksgiving: Most everyone needs a good "atta boy" from time to time to feel appreciated. But that's not why we thank God for things. He doesn't need our thanks to feel worthwhile (just as he doesn't need our adoration to boost his self-esteem). As with the elements of adoration and confession, thanksgiving is an integral part of prayer because *we* need to be reminded that God is the source of all we have and all good things.

"S" is for supplication: Sorry. We got stuck using this word—supplication—because it makes the acronym work. Although it sounds a bit churchy, supplication simply means talking to God about our own needs and the needs of others. This is where our prayers touch upon our desires for God to do certain things in our life—things we need or want. God has that omniscience thing working for him, so he does not need to hear our prayers in order to know our thoughts:

O Lord, you have examined my heart and know everything about me. You know when I sit down or stand up. You know my every thought when far away. You chart the path ahead of me and tell me where to stop and rest. Every moment you know where I am. You know what I am going to say even before I say it, Lord.

PSALM 139:1-4

The purpose of supplication is not to inform God about what is important to us. It is to allow us to express these concerns in the context of being submissive to his sovereign plan for our lives.

If your prayers begin with adoration and move through confession and thanksgiving *before* you start talking to God about what you want, you are more likely to align your will to his instead of insisting that he do things your way. That is the purpose of prayer: to bring you to a deeper, intimate relationship with God so that you know his thoughts and desires.

The Dynamic Interplay Between
Our Prayers and God's Providence

Now that we have reviewed a few basics about prayer, let's get to some specific points that relate to praying for specific results:

1. Don't pray with the sole intent of changing God's mind.

We might think that our eloquence—or our pleading—persuades God to change his mind about the circumstances of our life. But it doesn't always work like that.

The Bible teaches that God's plan is fixed and definite, but yet the Bible also teaches that our prayers concerning God's plan have value (see James 5:16). As theologian Millard J. Erickson explains, God works in sort of a partnership with man: God may not act if man doesn't do his part. Conversely, God may respond to prayers in a manner that accomplishes the results that are consistent with the plan he had all along. Sometimes the Bible describes these situations as prayers that "changed God's mind" (as in Deuteronomy 9:7-19 when God was going to obliterate the Israelites for worshipping the golden calf, but Moses prayed for them to be spared and God deferred to Moses' request).

But don't expect that you'll persuade God to your way of thinking every time you pray about something. First of all, our prayers never add to God's knowledge. He never says, "Oh, my! I never realized that. Thanks for telling me. That information completely changes my mind about what I was going to do." No, God has known all along everything there is to know.

Secondly, God is not going to be persuaded to opt for some alternate plan that is less than the best. His judgment is infallible, and no amount of whining on our part is going to wear down his resistance so that he gives us something other than his best. (That whining approach may have worked on our parents when we were teenagers, but God is impervious to such ploys.)

2. Our prayers are effective in accomplishing God's purposes.

Although our prayers don't change God's mind, that doesn't mean that they are superfluous and, therefore, worthless. Quite the contrary. The Bible clearly teaches that our prayers play an effective role in how God works:

> *The earnest prayer of a righteous person has great power and wonderful results.*

JAMES 5:16

Here's how it works: Our prayers help us get in tune with God's will. When we are in sync with his will, our prayers *release* the will of God (see John 9:31). Prayer is the most effective means to release the will of God. He hears every prayer made in accordance with his will, and acts upon it:

> *And we can be confident that he will listen to us whenever we ask him for anything in line with his will. And if we know he is listening when we make our requests, we can be sure that he will give us what we ask for.*

1 JOHN 5:14-15

Thus, prayer does not change what God has planned to do, but it is the triggering device by which he releases the power to accomplish what he planned.

3. God wants us praying—all the time, about everything.

When we are praying according to God's will for the circumstances of our life, we can have the confidence that God will give us all we need. Of course, it is easy for us to slip out of that mindset and become selfish and self-centered. Maybe that's why God wants us to be in a constant state of prayer. Mealtimes and bedtimes are not enough. He wants us to be in a continual attitude of prayer so that we experience all of the events of our lives with the proper perspective of his will:

> *Pray at all times and on every occasion in the power of the Holy Spirit.*
>
> EPHESIANS 6:18

Jesus told his disciples that they were to be persistent in their prayers. The language of Luke 11:8-10 says it this way: keep asking, keep seeking, keep knocking. When we are persistent and intent in our prayers, then we stay focused in living within the context of God's plan. Even though we may not know the specifics of that plan, our prayers remind us that God knows what is best for us. With the assurance of that fact, then we don't need to sweat the specifics because we know that God's got them covered:

> *Don't worry about anything; instead, pray about everything. Tell God what you need, and thank him for all he has done. If you do this, you will experience God's peace, which is far more wonderful than the human mind can understand. His peace will guard your hearts and minds as you live in Christ Jesus.*
>
> PHILIPPIANS 4:6-7

4. We do not always receive what we ask for.
You probably already knew this. But maybe you'll feel better to know that you aren't the only one whose prayers have been denied by God. Paul prayed three times for God to take away a certain problem in his life. Each time the request was denied, but God gave to Paul something that was more important for him to have at the time:

> *Three different times I begged the Lord to take it away. Each time he said, "My gracious favor is all you need. My power works best in your weakness." So now I am glad to boast about my weaknesses, so that the power of Christ*

may work through me. Since I know it is all for Christ's good, I am quite content with my weaknesses.

2 CORINTHIANS 12:8-10

And just so you know that God doesn't play favorites, he denied the requests that Jesus made—three times—in the Garden of Gethsemane to be spared the death of crucifixion if it was possible. It wasn't possible, because the death of Christ on the cross was an integral part of God's salvation plan.

Don't worry about praying for the wrong thing. There is no "wrong thing" so long as you are praying in the context of preferring God's will to your own. Even if your current preferences are not precisely aligned with what God has in mind, that's OK. He won't give it to you just because you are asking for it. But he will give you what you need. It may not necessarily be what you ask for, but it will be what is best for you.

No good thing will the Lord withhold from those who do what is right.

PSALM 84:11

Praying God's Will

Prayer is, in large part, a matter of creating within ourselves a right attitude about God's will. Jesus emphasized this principle in the model prayer he gave to his disciples (often referred to as the "Lord's Prayer").

In this prayer, the request for personal needs ("Give us our food for today") is preceded by a statement of overall submission to God's will ("May your will be done here on earth, just as it is in heaven"). Prayer is not so much a means of getting God to do our will as it is a way of demonstrating to God (and reminding ourselves) that we want his will to be done.

Bible scholar R.C. Sproul has grappled with the concepts of God's sovereignty and providence, and in *The Invisible Hand* he offers this summary about the role of prayer in seeking God's will:

In prayer we have the opportunity to learn of the character of the Father. Indeed, prayer is one of the most effective means we have to discern the invisible hand of Providence. The more we understand the character of God, the easier it is for us to see His hand at work in our lives.... When we are praying in general we tend to see the work of Providence likewise "in general." When we pray specifically we begin to be overwhelmed by the specific answers to our prayer that vividly display His hand to us. By this our faith is strengthened, and our confidence in His Providence is intensified.[4]

Read the last sentence of Sproul's quote again. That's what extreme living is all about. You overcome any obstacles and you can enjoy life to the fullest when you have intense confidence in God's plan. Prayer plays an important part in strengthening your faith to that point.

In the next chapter we will look at the stories of several individuals who had unusual faith. As you will see, their faith in God's plan was so intense that they each enjoyed the adventure of living an extreme life.

CHAPTER 11

Lead, Follow,
and Get Out of the Way

Well, how much more do I need to say? It would take too long to recount the stories of the faith of Gideon, Barak, Samson, Jephthah, David, Samuel, and all the prophets. By faith these people overthrew kingdoms, ruled with justice, and received what God had promised them.

—Hebrews 11:32-33

This chapter of Hebrews reads like God's "Hall of Fame for Extreme Living." These men and women of faith overcame great obstacles—including their own shortcomings—to do great things for God. Each of these people have three things in common:

1. They allowed God to **lead.**
2. They inspired others to **follow.**
3. They subordinated their own agendas to God's plans, and kept their hearts clean before God so they could hear him clearly. (They **got out of the way.**)

These three qualities are summed up in Hebrews 11:6:

So, you see, it is impossible to please God without faith. Anyone who wants to come to him must believe that there is a God and that he rewards those who sincerely seek him.

Let's take a look at some of the people named in this "Hall of Fame" chapter. What do their lives say to us today about living life to the extreme?

Abraham: All I Have Is Yours, God

Abraham had it all. Flocks and tents and servants and family and ... wait. Skip that last one. Although God had promised Abraham that one day his progeny would be "too many to count" (Genesis 15:5), for most of their married life Sarah was unable to have children. Finally, when Abraham was one hundred years old, Sarah became pregnant and had a son, Isaac (see Genesis 21:1-7).

Now Abraham's joy was complete. Complete, but short-lived. It wasn't long before God spoke to Abraham again:

Take your son, your only son—yes, Isaac, whom you love so much—and go to the land of Moriah. Sacrifice him there as a burnt offering on one of the mountains, which I will point out to you.

GENESIS 22:2

Imagine what you would have done if you had been in Abraham's sandals. (If you don't already know what happened, check out the story in Genesis 22.) Hebrews 11 tells us the reason Abraham was able to make this kind of sacrifice: He figured that if Isaac died, God would bring him back from the dead. Talk about faith!

Think about it. Have you ever felt God was asking you to sacrifice something that was very precious to you? It could be a relationship, a dream, or even a seemingly harmless habit. It might not make sense—and could be very painful—at the time. And God might not spare you from making that sacrifice, as he did with Abraham and Isaac. At the same time, we can hold on to the promise of Jesus:

> *I assure you that everyone who has given up house or brothers or sisters or mother or father or children or property, for my sake and for the Good News, will receive now in return, a hundred times over, houses, brothers, sisters, mothers, children, and property—with persecutions. And in the world to come they will have eternal life.*
>
> MARK 10:29-30

In the story of Abraham, we find an important principle about "extreme living":

**Receive what God gives you gratefully,
but don't hold on too tight.**

Barak: Two Heads Are Better Than One

We read about Barak in the fourth chapter of Judges. During this time in Israel's history, the people were ruled by judges rather than kings—and in Judges 4:4-5, we find that a woman, Deborah, is holding court under the palm trees.

One day Deborah sends for Barak and tells him to assemble the troops and go after Sisera, the commander of King Jabin's army. (As we see in Judges 4:2, God had punished the Israelites for their disobedience by "handing them over" to this Canaanite king.)

Barak feels a bit unsure of himself where Sisera is concerned and tells Deborah, "I will go, but only if you go with me!"

Now, not many men would have requested this. Deborah may have been a prophetess, but she was, after all, a woman! However, Barak had faith in God and understood that having God's blessing was more important than personal glory.

This story gives us another hint about what it takes to live life in all its fullness:

If you're unsure of what to do, get the support of someone who listens to God!

Jephthah: Beware of Rash Promises

A little later in the Book of Judges, we read about another of Israel's judges, Jephthah of Gilead (see Judges 11). Now, this guy does not have the most impressive background. His mother was a prostitute, and his father's wife had several sons who ran him out of town so he couldn't get his hands on any of their inheritance.

However, this guy was not one to hold a grudge, and he later returned home to help his people win against the Ammonites. To ensure victory, Jephthah made a vow to the Lord: The first thing coming out of his house to greet him upon his return would be sacrificed to the Lord (see Judges 11:31).

To Jephthah's horror, the first creature to run out of his house in greeting was not a pet lamb. It was his only daughter. And Jephthah was stuck. He had made a promise to God. God had kept his part of the bargain. Now what?

Unfortunately, this story does not have a happy ending, like the Abraham story. You can read about it in Judges 11:34-40. However, it does suggest an important principle about living life to the extreme:

Hasty decisions and rash promises can bring real heartache down the road.

David: Trusting God at Every Turn

From the time he was a young shepherd boy fending off Goliath with a slingshot, David was someone who epitomized "living to the extreme." Whether he was making music or ruling a nation, King David never forgot the source of his strength: his friendship with God.

All you have to do is read through the Psalms to catch a glimpse of the intimacy he had with the Creator of the Universe:

The king proclaims the Lord's decree:
"The Lord said to me, 'You are my son. Today I have become your
*   Father.*
Only ask, and I will give you the nations as your inheritance,
the ends of the earth as your possession.'"

PSALM 2:7-8

I love you, Lord; you are my strength.
The Lord is my rock, my fortress, and my savior....
I will call on the Lord, who is worthy of praise,
for he saves me from my enemies.

PSALM 18:1-2,3

How long, O Lord, will you look on and do nothing?
Rescue me from their fierce attacks.
Protect my life from these lions!

PSALM 35:17

As the deer pants for streams of water,
so I long for you, O God.

PSALM 42:1

I took my troubles to the Lord;
I cried out to him, and he answered my prayer.

PSALM 120:1

In these psalms (and others like them,) David shows us another principle of extreme living:

God can be trusted with what we think and feel.
When no one else cares, God does.

Jairus and the Woman Who Touched Jesus' Hem: Seekers Reaching Out for God

Although these two people are not named in the "Hall of Fame" chapter of Hebrews, clearly they made an impression on Jesus: two of the four Gospels record their stories (see Matthew 9:18-26; Luke 8:43-56).

Jairus was the leader of a local synagogue. His only child was dying, a twelve-year-old girl. Rumors had been circulating about this miracle-worker from Nazareth, and the girl's father ran to where Jesus was and begged him to heal his daughter. And so Jesus went with him.

Now remember, this was a big risk for Jairus. He had his reputation to consider, his position in the community and in the synagogue. But when faced with losing one of the people he loved most in this world, the choice was clear. Nothing else mattered. And because of his faith, his child was restored to complete health.

The second person, the woman who had been bleeding for twelve years, is not named in the Gospel account. She was on the other end of the social scale: Because of her condition, she would have been considered "unclean" for the duration of the bleeding, unfit for regular society. She did not even speak to Jesus—she felt that unworthy. And yet Jesus immediately knew what she had done. He spoke to her, restoring her dignity as a human being; and he healed her, restoring her to physical wholeness.

This account reminds us that it's not always the person who does "extreme" things who receives the fullness of life in Christ. Sometimes it's the person who just faithfully serves where he (or she) is planted, like

Jairus—someone whose faith is lived out quietly for the most part but is readily apparent at the critical moment.

For other people, living life to the extreme means never giving up, even in the face of overwhelming obstacles. It means continually reaching out to God even though you feel like you don't deserve it, and trusting him to give you the strength to make it through the day. It's as Paul proclaims in Romans 8:35,37:

> *Can anything ever separate us from Christ's love? Does it mean he no longer loves us if we have trouble or calamity, or are persecuted, or are hungry or cold or in danger or threatened with death?... No, despite all these things, overwhelming victory is ours through Christ, who loved us!*

As we head into the final chapter, consider the stories of these "Hall of Fame" Christians. How do their experiences relate to what's going on in your life?

CHAPTER 12

When God Taps You
on the Shoulder

*As God's obedient child, you are in a love relationship with
him. He loves you and wants to involve you in his work.
When he is ready, he will show you where
he is working so you can join him.*

—Henry Blackaby and Claude King

What makes a person great? We want to ask this question as our book draws to a close because greatness and living life to the extreme are closely related. You have hung around with us for eleven chapters and learned a lot about what it means to live life to the extreme by making choices that matter. We sense that you are ready to go out there and do something great in the world, but first we need to ask if greatness is defined by the things you do, or is it measured by the person you are?

Some people use accomplishments as the standard for greatness because they're easier to measure. Columbus discovered America, Neil Armstrong walked on the moon, the Beatles changed popular music, Michael Jordan won six NBA championships, Mother Teresa worked with the sick in

Calcutta: these are the people we remember as great because of what they accomplished, either in a moment or a lifetime.

Other people insist on defining greatness by a person's inner qualities. This is a little trickier, because how do you measure character? How do you compare one person's integrity with another's? You can't see great inner qualities. There are no barriers to cross, as in science, and no records to break, as in sports. So how do you know when you have enough character to be great? Certainly people of great character can accomplish great things (Mother Teresa is an example), but great things can also be accomplished by people of questionable character.

God's Idea of Greatness

You will be interested to know that the Bible has some direct advice about what it means to be great. On one occasion the disciples asked Jesus about who would be the greatest in heaven, and he answered by calling a child over to him. Then he said:

Therefore, anyone who becomes as humble as this little child is the greatest.

MATTHEW 18:4

Another time Jesus spoke to his disciples and a large crowd and said:

The greatest among you must be a servant.

MATTHEW 23:12

There you have it. If you want to be great, you have to concentrate on both things. You need to have an attitude of humility (this is who you are), and you need to serve others (this is what you do). As usual, Jesus did not simply offer wise advice. He lived it. Jesus gave us these two components of greatness because this is exactly what he did. The apostle Paul explains how

Jesus combined the attitude of humility with the action of serving.

> *Your attitude should be the same that Christ Jesus had. Though he was God, he did not demand and cling to his rights as God. He made himself nothing; he took the humble position of a slave and appeared in human form. And in human form he obediently humbled himself even further by dying a criminal's death on a cross.*
>
> PHILIPPIANS 2:5-8

This is God's idea of greatness, and this is the attitude he wants us to have. If you wonder whether humility and service will lead to greatness, read what happened to Jesus:

> *Because of this, God raised him up to the heights of heaven and gave him a name that is above every name, so that at the name of Jesus every knee will bow, in heaven and on earth and under the earth, and every tongue will confess that Jesus Christ is Lord, to the glory of God the Father.*
>
> PHILIPPIANS 2:9-11

The reason God wants us to have the same attitude that Jesus had is because when we are humble and when we serve, we are in the place where God can use us to accomplish great things for him. Think about it. When you're humble and when you serve, two things happen. First, you get quiet so you can tune in to what is going on around you. Second, you become other-centered (instead of self-centered). This is where God wants you, because now you're in a position where God can lead you to greatness. There are three reasons for this.

You Will Listen to God

When you're quiet and you take the attention off yourself, you will listen to God. A lot of us make the mistake of thinking that God will catch up with us in our extremely busy lives, tackle us from behind and say, "Now stop and listen to me. I've got something to say to you!"

No, God doesn't work that way. God won't compete with your schedule or your running around, even if you're doing "his work." It's only in those moments of quiet and calm that he will speak to us.

Be silent, and know that I am God!

PSALM 46:10

C'mon, God created the universe—can't he get our attention any other way? We sometimes have this image of God as some Supreme Being who hurls lightning bolts to get our attention. However, God prefers to speak when he has our quiet, undivided attention. Sometimes that happens when we're flat on our backs with an illness or at the end of our ropes in a crisis or at the bottom of the barrel financially. God isn't picky about our quiet moments, as long as we are humble before him and focused on others and on him.

Umm ... I'd rather find another way to hear God's voice. Any ideas? If you want to hear God's voice, it's best to choose a time and place during a quiet time in your schedule each day. God speaks to us in a number of ways, but primarily he speaks through the Bible—and through your prayers. Did you know that God speaks through your prayers? Here's what Henry Blackaby and Claude King wrote in *Experiencing God:*

> Prayer is two-way fellowship and communication with God. You speak to God and He speaks to you. It's not a one-way conversation. Your personal prayer life may primarily be one-way communication—you talking to God. Prayer is more than that. Prayer includes listening as well. In fact, what God says in prayer is far more important than what you say.[5]

As you become disciplined in meeting God daily in your "quiet time," you will begin to appreciate this as the most important and powerful part of your day. Rather than dreading Bible study and prayer as "boring" or unproductive, you will find yourself cherishing this time, because this is when God will give you his vision and his purpose for your life.

You Will Know God's Purpose

When you take the attention off yourself and listen to God, you will know God's purpose for you.

God's daily purpose for your life. What does God want you to do in the next twenty-four hours? Obviously, he wants you to do those things he has asked you to do in his Word:

- Love God with all your heart, soul and mind (see Matthew 22:37).
- Love your neighbor as yourself (see Matthew 22:39).
- Live wisely and take every opportunity to do good (see Ephesians 5:15-16).
- Respect your husband (see Ephesians 5:24).
- Love your wife (see Ephesians 5:25).
- Honor your father and mother (see Ephesians 6:2).
- Serve your employer as you would serve Christ (see Ephesians 6:5).
- Treat your employees fairly and with respect (see Ephesians 6:9).

Now, you don't have to carry around a list each day so you can check off the times when you do these things (although some people would benefit from that). God wants you to do these things every day, but he wants them to come from an attitude of love and service, not obligation and selfishness.

God's greater purpose for your life. This is what Gerald Sittser calls "the big picture of his redemptive plan." This is purpose on a cosmic scale, bigger and farther reaching than we can even imagine, yet he wants each one of us to be involved. Before you became a Christian, this big purpose was a mystery. But now that you know God and you are growing in your knowledge of who he is and what he wants you to do, he is showing you what that purpose is.

God's secret plan has now been revealed to us; it is a plan centered on Christ, designed long ago according to his good pleasure. And this is his plan: At the right time he will bring everything together under the authority of Christ— everything in heaven and on earth.

EPHESIANS 1:9-10

God's greater purpose is to seek and to save those who are lost without Christ. "God did not send his Son into the world to condemn it, but to save it" (John 3:17). Many people have the mistaken notion that God can't wait to send people to hell. That's not God's purpose. God doesn't want anyone to die in sin. In fact, he is being patient and giving the world more time than it deserves so "everyone can repent" (2 Peter 3:9).

His greater purpose for those who have already responded by choosing Christ is to tell others about God's plan. It's as simple as that. How we accomplish that purpose isn't as simple, but it sure is exciting.

You Will Work Where God Is at Work

As you take the attention off yourself, listen to God, and discover God's purpose for you, then you will begin to work where God is at work. If you are too wrapped up in your own activities and goals, it's hard to see anything else. You may even be working in an area where you are convinced God wants you to be. But there's a much better way to go. Rather than asking God to join you in your work, God wants you to join him in his work. This doesn't mean that your work is insignificant. You just can't match God. All you can do is join him.

Does this mean that you need to pack your bags and move to Bosnia, after all? Probably not. It does mean, however, you need to adjust your priorities to match God's priorities, to live your life in a way that reflects the love and life of Christ to those around you. That's what it means to live life to the extreme.

As we close this book, we'd like to offer you twelve principles you will want to keep in mind as you pursue the life God wants you to have: Real Life to the Extreme.

12 Principles for Real Life to the Extreme

1. Remember, extreme living is a marathon, not a sprint. If you stumble along the way, pick yourself up and start over. Like the apostle Paul said in his Second Letter to Timothy (4:7-8):

> *I have fought a good fight, I have finished the race, and I have remained faithful. And now the prize awaits me—the crown of righteousness that the Lord, the righteous Judge, will give me on that great day of his return.*

Ask God for the strength to help you run the race to win!

2. Cultivate a "support network." It's important to have some people in your life who will encourage you to stay on course and push you to do better. They could be friends, family, mentors, heroes—even enemies. Some you should consult on a regular basis, and others you may see only once in a while. Paul and Timothy admonish the Christians in Colossi (Colossians 3:12-13,16):

> *Since God chose you to be the holy people whom he loves, you must clothe yourselves with tenderhearted mercy, kindness, humility, gentleness, and patience. You must make allowance for each other's faults and forgive the person who offends you.... Let the words of Christ, in all their richness, live in your hearts and make you wise. Use his words to teach and counsel each other.*

3. Saturate your mind and heart in the Word of God. The people you meet in the pages of Scripture weren't perfect people—far from it. But their hearts were passionate for God.

Moses was one of history's greatest leaders. He was George Washington and Abraham Lincoln rolled into one. Imagine being Joshua, who served as Moses' assistant. You're the number-two person living in the shadow of a very popular Number One. Then one day God taps you on the shoulder and says it's your time to lead. Or maybe he asks you to do something that seems way beyond you. How do you handle it? Simple. You focus on God by staying in his Word. You follow the advice God gave to Joshua:

Study this Book of the Law continually. Meditate on it day and night so you may be sure to obey all that is written in it. Only then will you succeed.

JOSHUA 1:8

4. Walk closely with God and do what he says. Most people remember Noah for the huge floating zoo he built to escape the Flood. But God remembers Noah for quite another reason. Here's what the Bible says about him:

Noah was a righteous man, the only blameless man living on earth at the time. He consistently followed God's will and enjoyed a close relationship with him.

GENESIS 6:9

What a fabulous description, and it can be yours! OK, so you won't be the only righteous person in the world, but you can consistently follow God's will and enjoy a close relationship with him. It's not easy, but it's doable. Ask God to help you take him seriously and do what he says—whether it's building an ark or witnessing to a friend.

5. Trust God for the results, even when the odds are against you. If you ever feel as if you've been wronged or the world is against you (you may feel like that now), study the life of Joseph. This poor guy experienced more ups and downs than the stock market.

- His father singled him out by giving him a designer jacket, and then his brothers sold him into slavery.
- He found favor with a high-ranking government official, and then the official's wife lied about his character, leading to his imprisonment.

- Finally, God redeemed Joseph and elevated him to the second highest position in Egypt so he could accomplish something great for God. Even in his darkest hour, Joseph was faithful to God. He never lost sight of the big picture, even when the smaller pieces didn't make sense. Joseph lived by this statement, made to his brothers, and so can you:

As far as I am concerned, God turned into good what you meant for evil. He brought me to the high position I have today so I could save the lives of many people.

GENESIS 50:20

6. Work on your character more than your appearance. When you think of David, Israel's greatest king, you think of a hero and a legend, someone bigger than life.

Had you met David and seen him face-to-face, you may have been tempted to change your opinion. In physical appearance, David was more like Pee-Wee Herman than Arnold Schwarzenegger. He was short and ruddy, and the people of Israel wanted a king who was tall, dark, and handsome—it's why they had asked for Saul in the first place! This time, they asked the prophet Samuel to appoint Saul. God had another idea.

But the Lord said to Samuel, "Don't judge by his appearance or height, for I have rejected him. The Lord doesn't make decisions the way you do! People judge by outward appearance, but the Lord looks at a person's thoughts and intentions."

1 SAMUEL 16:7

God is more interested in the heart than the head, and here's where David was a true hero. Despite his many flaws, David had a heart for God throughout his life. He paid more attention to his attitude than his appearance.

7. Respond to God's direction even if it's painful. Old Testament prophets were a peculiar people. Colorful, crusty, somewhat ill-tempered (you would be too if you spent your life telling people to repent), they frequently heard from God directly. Isaiah is perhaps the best-known Old Testament prophet because his book erupts with dramatic predictions and sobering instructions. The way God called Isaiah is instructive for us, and not because any of us will become prophets. The lesson is that God may have to do some character shaping before he can use us, and that may be painful. Here's what happened to Isaiah:

> *Then one of the seraphim flew over to the altar, and he picked up a burning coal with a pair of tongs. He touched my lips with it and said, "See, this coal has touched your lips. Now your guilt is removed, and your sins are forgiven." Then I heard the Lord asking, "Whom should I send as a messenger to my people? Who will go for us?" And I said, "Lord, I'll go! Send me."*
>
> ISAIAH 6:6-8

Isaiah endured the pain of the burning coal as a means of purification. Your pain may be physical, like Isaiah's, or God may choose to purify you through a different kind of crisis. God will use whatever means necessary to work on your character so you can do his work.

8. No matter how old you are, God can use you. Jeremiah was another great prophet. God asked Jeremiah to do his work when he was still very young. In fact, this troubled Jeremiah, and he raised his youth as an objection. God responded with a message in which we can all take comfort:

> *"I knew you before I formed you in your mother's womb. Before you were born I set you apart and appointed you as my spokesman to the world."*
>
> *"O Sovereign Lord," I said, "I can't speak for you! I am too young!"*
>
> *"Don't say that," the Lord replied, "for you must go wherever I send you and say whatever I tell you."*
>
> JEREMIAH 1:4-7

Having some age and experience with God has its advantages, but more critical is your desire to experience God. Don't feel overwhelmed and under-qualified just because you are young or lack experience as a Christian. Just like Jeremiah, God may tap you on the shoulder, even if you just started shaving. He may ask you to do something great while you're still in college. God can ask you to lead a company before you hit thirty. Age doesn't matter to God. What he wants is a will that conforms to his will and a heart that follows his.

9. Do your best to gain the confidence of those in authority over you.
There came a time in Israel's history when God needed someone to manage a big construction project. The walls around Jerusalem had crumbled beyond repair, and he needed someone to take on the gargantuan job of rebuilding them. God needed someone to convince the king to help.

God chose Nehemiah for a couple of reasons. First, Nehemiah had a heart for God; second, Nehemiah had gained the favor of the king. Nehemiah lived a life of such exemplary character and skill that even the king, who had no interest in God, took notice. Nehemiah was as well known in the community as he was in the church. He lived a life of integrity and excellence in both arenas, so when he asked the king for some big favors (protection, building materials, financing, etc.), the king granted the requests because the "gracious hand of God" was on Nehemiah (Nehemiah 2:8).

God wants us to serve each other in love, but he doesn't want it to stop there. We need to serve those in authority over us so we can gain their favor. We need to be the best businesspeople, scientists, athletes, teachers, musicians, computer experts, designers, and writers possible so the "kings" of our world will notice us and help us. God uses secular leaders as well as sacred saints. If we are going to have an impact in our culture—if our voice is going to be heard—we need to gain the favor of those who can help us work where God is working.

10. Be willing to stand in the gap. The story of Esther reads like a Hollywood script. There's a royal romance, intrigue, deception, irony and suspense. There are good guys and bad guys (and the good guys win).

For our purposes, the lesson of Queen Esther's life is that she was willing to do what God asked, even though she had to risk her own reputation and her life. She listened to God, and she listened to her adviser, who said:

> *What's more, who can say but that you have been elevated to the palace for just such a time as this?*
>
> ESTHER 4:14

Doesn't that inspire you? Wouldn't you enjoy the thrill—if only once in your life—of standing in the gap for God "for such a time as this"? Now, that's living life to the extreme!

11. God will give you his power through the Holy Spirit. Mary, the mother of Jesus, is one of the most celebrated figures in the Bible. You know the story: An ordinary teenage girl, engaged to a carpenter, is picking out pottery patterns for her wedding. Then one night the angel Gabriel comes to Mary and tells the virgin that she is going to have a son—not from Joseph but from the Holy Spirit. And he won't be just any son, but the Son of God (see Luke 1:30-33).

Understandably, Mary is confused and probably a little frightened. This was extreme! Then the angel assures Mary that God will give her all the power necessary to get the job done.

> *The angel replied, "The Holy Spirit will come upon you, and the power of the Most High will overshadow you."*
>
> LUKE 1:35

Never forget that the ability and the power to be who God wants you to be, and to do what God wants you to do, comes from him.

12. God will use you even if you blow it. A lot of people think that God could never use them, either because they've lived a rotten life or because they've done something very bad. They think that God recruits people for his work based on an application that says: "If you have a criminal record or you have done something really stupid, you are disqualified from serving the Lord."

The truth is, there are only two qualifications to be used by God. One, you must have a personal relationship with Jesus. Two, you need to ask God's forgiveness when you blow it.

If you have any doubts about this, check out the life of the apostle Peter. He blew it several times (that we know about from the Bible), and none bigger than the time he denied Jesus right before the crucifixion. But Peter asked forgiveness, and God used him in a powerful way. Peter was the most passionate preacher of the early church and its first leader.

Of all the things you take from this book, this last point may be the most important. Hey, we've all blown it, so don't think for a minute that God only uses perfect people (if that were the case, he wouldn't use anyone). Truth is, God is very big on second chances (and third and fourth chances). He wants you just as you are, willing to be used by him and ready to live your life to the extreme for him.

Why settle for the temporary thrills the world has to offer when you can live a life of adventure for God? Pursue a real life—to the extreme! You'll never regret it.

NOTES

1. **Robert Jastrow,** *God and the Astonomers* (New York: W.W. Norton, 1992), 9-10.

2. **Wayne Grudem,** *Systematic Theology* (Grand Rapids, Mich: Zondervan, 1994), 440-41.

3. **Gerald Sittser,** *The Will of God as a Way of Life: Finding and Following the Will of God* (Grand Rapids, Mich: Zondervan, 2000), 29.

4. **R.C. Sproul,** *The Invisible Hand: Do All Things Really Work for Good?* (Dallas, Tex.: Word, 1996), 207.

5. **Henry T. Blackaby and Claude V. King,** *Experiencing God: How to Live the Full Adventure of Knowing and Doing the Will of God* (Nashville, Tenn.: Broadman and Holman, 1994), 174.

BIBLIOGRAPHY

Bickel, Bruce, and Stan Jantz. *Bruce & Stan's Pocket Guide to Talking with God.* Eugene, Ore.: Harvest House, 2000.

Blackaby, Henry T. and Claude V. King. *Experiencing God: How to Live the Full Adventure of Knowing and Doing the Will of God.* Nashville, Tenn.: Broadman & Holman, 1994.

Campolo, Tony. *Carpe Diem: Seize the Day.* Dallas: Word, 1994.

Erickson, Millard J. *Christian Theology.* Grand Rapids, Mich.: Baker Book House, 1983.

Friesen, Garry and Robin Maxon. *Decision Making and the Will of God.* Sisters, Ore.: Multonomah, 1980.

Grudem, Wayne. *Systematic Theology.* Grand Rapids, Mich.: Zondervan, 1994.

Johnston, Russ. *How to Know the Will of God.* Colorado Springs, Colo.: NavPress, 1980.

Lindsell, Harold and Charles J. Woodbridge. *A Handbook of Christian Truth.* Westwood, N.J.: Fleming H. Revell, 1953.

Little, Paul. *Affirming the Will of God.* Downers Grove, Ill.: InterVarsity Christian Fellowship, 1971.

MacArthur, John, Jr. *Found: God's Will.* Wheaton, Ill.: Victor Books, 1973.

Maxwell, John C. *Developing the Leader Within You.* Nashville, Tenn.: Thomas Nelson, 1993.

Morley, Patrick M. *The Rest of Your Life*. Nashville, Tenn.: Thomas Nelson, 1992.

Sittser, Gerald L. *The Will of God as a Way of Life: Finding and Following the Will of God*. Grand Rapids, Mich.: Zondervan, 2000.

Sproul, R.C. *The Invisible Hand: Do All Things Really Work for Good?*. Dallas: Word, 1996.

Swindoll, Charles R. *The Mystery of God's Will: What Does He Want for Me?* Nashville, Tenn.: Word, 1999.

White, John. *The Fight*. Downers Grove, Ill.: InterVarsity Press, 1976.

ABOUT THE AUTHORS

Bruce Bickel quickly abandoned his fledgling career as a comedian because he wasn't very funny. Now he is a probate lawyer, so everybody expects him to be boring. Bruce lives in Fresno, California, with his wife, Cheryl. When he isn't doing lawyer stuff, he is active at Westmont College, where he has taught and serves on the Board of Trustees.

Stan Jantz is the father part of a father-son business that designs and maintains Web sites for companies and nonprofit organizations. Stan lives in Fresno, California, with his wife, Karin. Stan is active in his church and is on the Board of Trustees at Biola Univeristy.

Bruce and Stan like to observe and comment on the culture around them. (It beats doing yard work and household chores). They must be noticing something because they have written twenty books that have sold more than 1.3 million copies.

Some of their popular books include:

Real Life Has No Expiration Date
Real Life Begins After High School
Bruce & Stan's Guide to God
Bruce & Stan's Guide to the Bible
Bruce & Stan's Guide to the End of the World
God Is in the Small Stuff—and It All Matters
God Is in the Small Stuff for Your Family
God Is in the Small Stuff for Your Marriage
God Is in the Small Stuff—Graduate's Edition

Bruce and Stan would enjoy hearing from you. You can contact them with your praise, your criticism (be gentle), and your comments or questions by E-mail at guide@bruceandstan.com. If you think they are worth the price of postage, you can send your letters and gifts to P.O. Box 25565, Fresno, CA 93729.

Their Web site address is: **www.bruceandstan.com** (Clever, huh?).